Centered

For Crayons And Wide Tipped Markers

Angie's Gentle Mood Menders

Volume 2

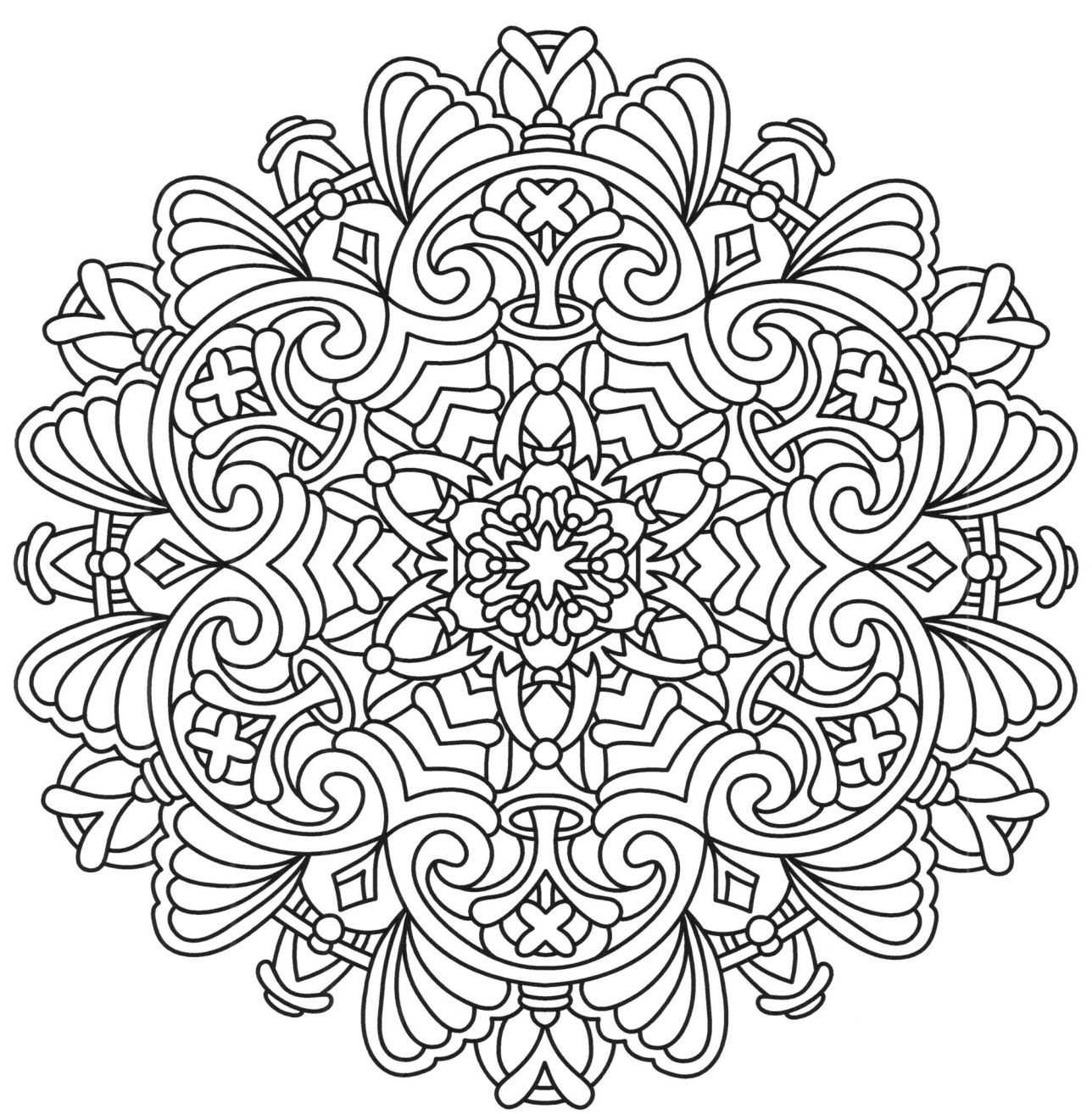

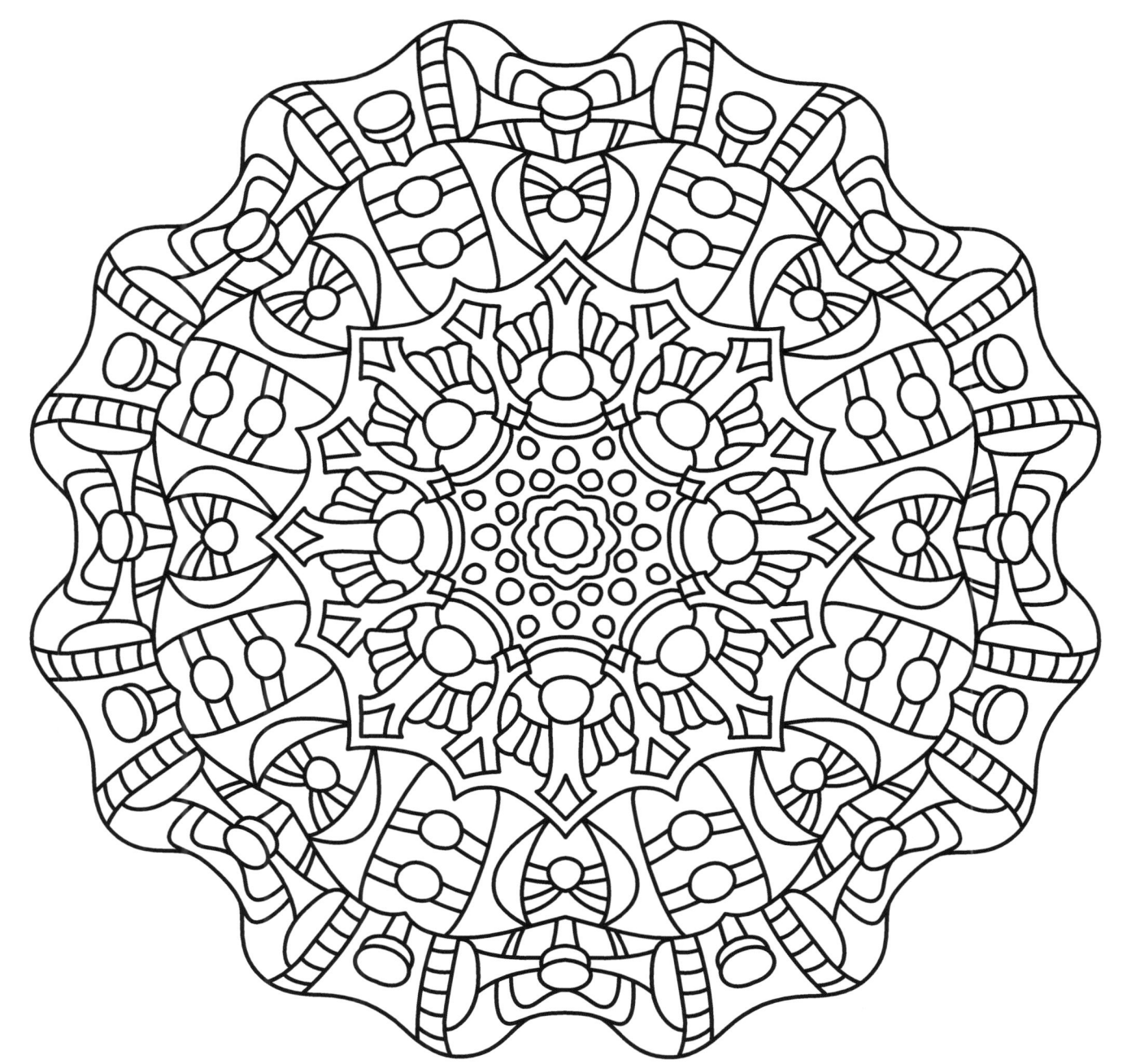

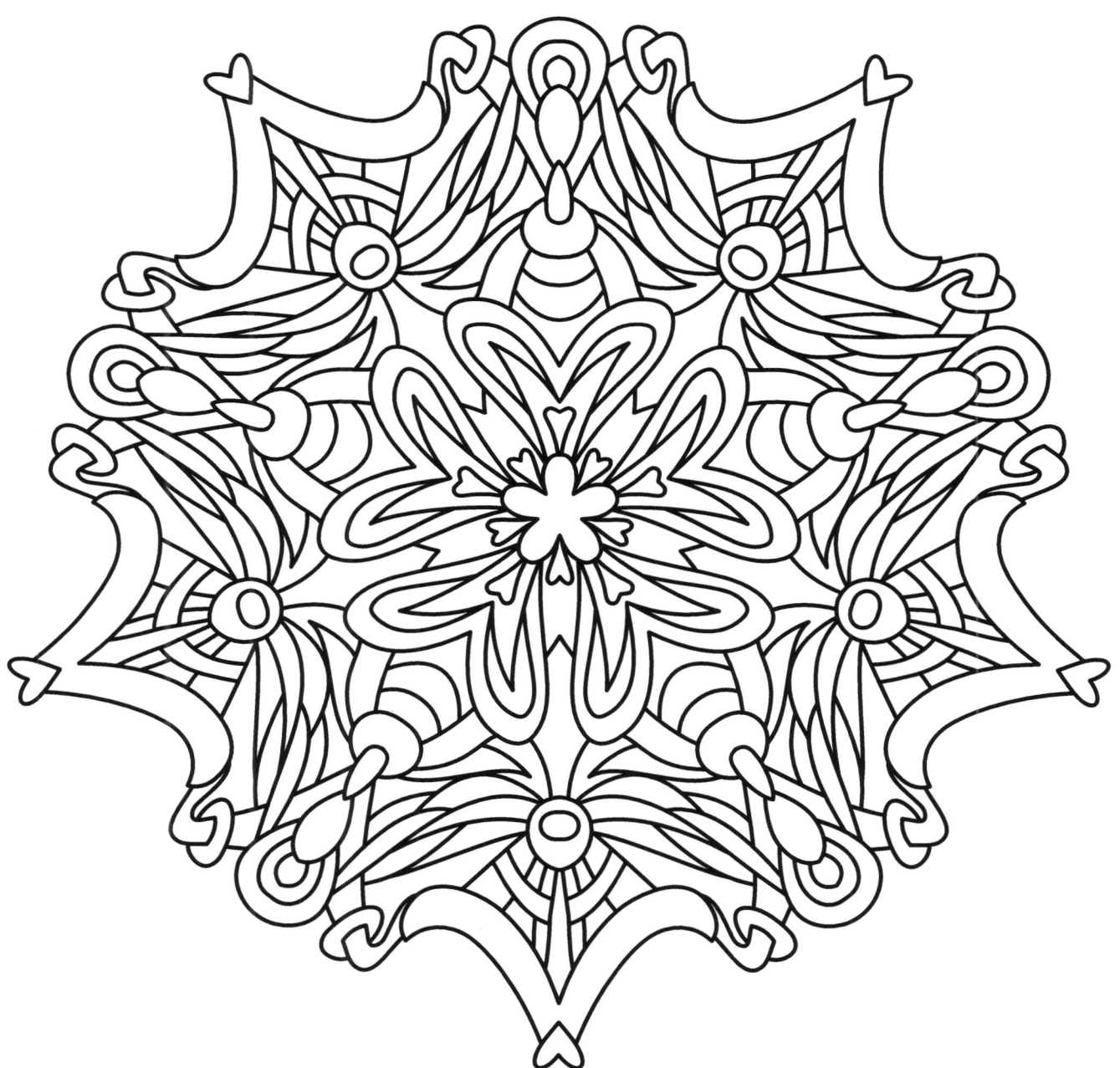

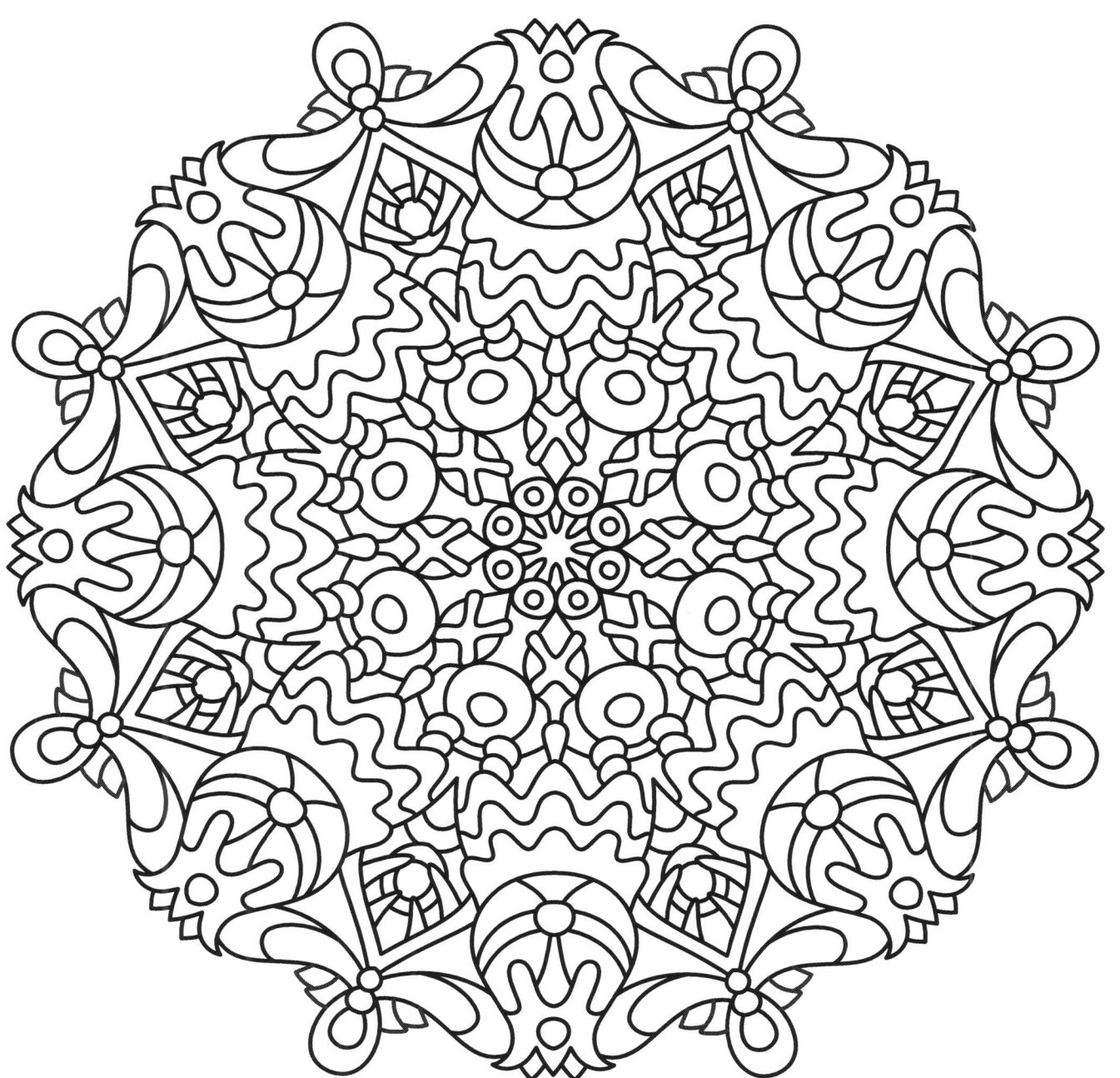

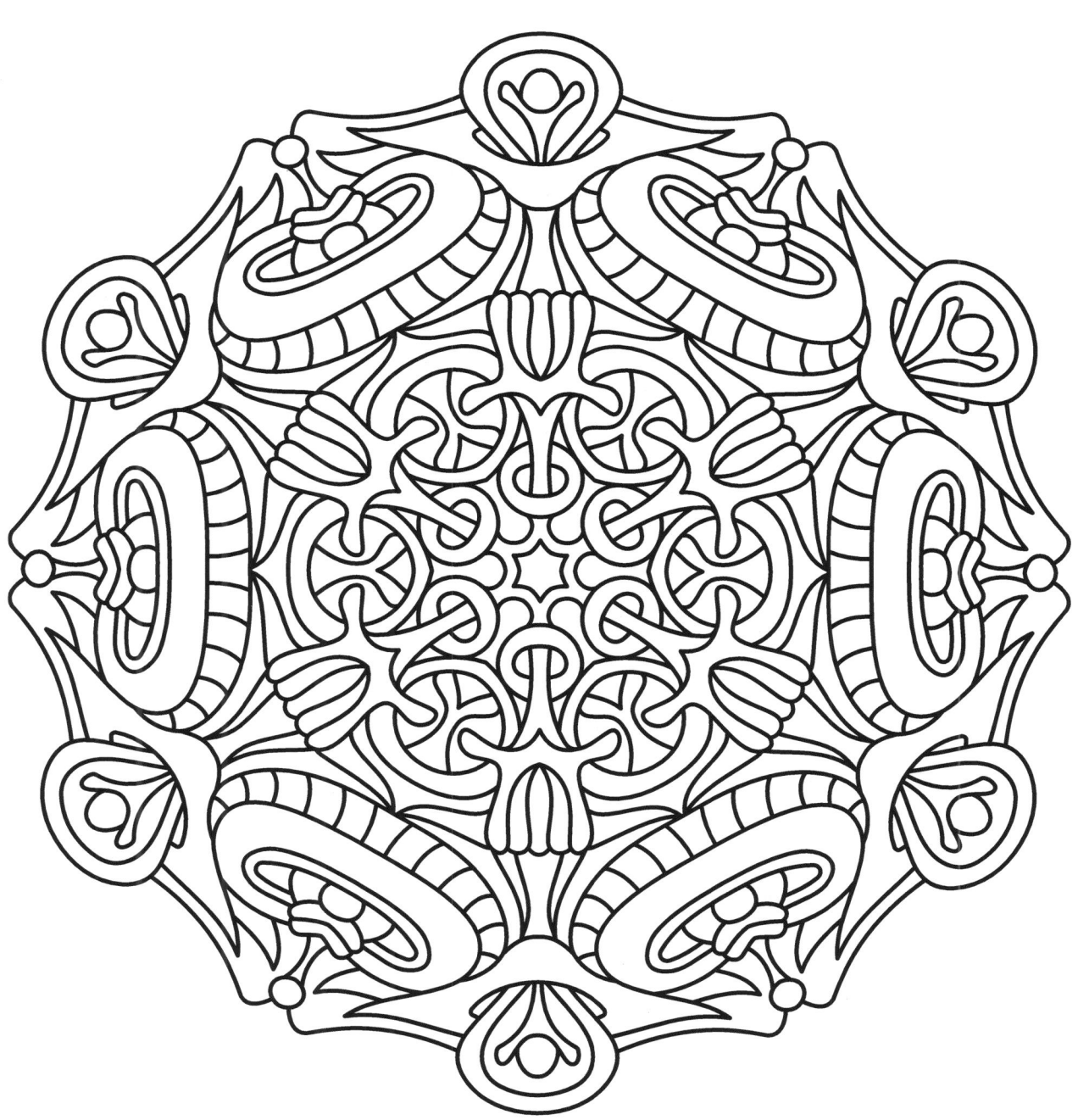

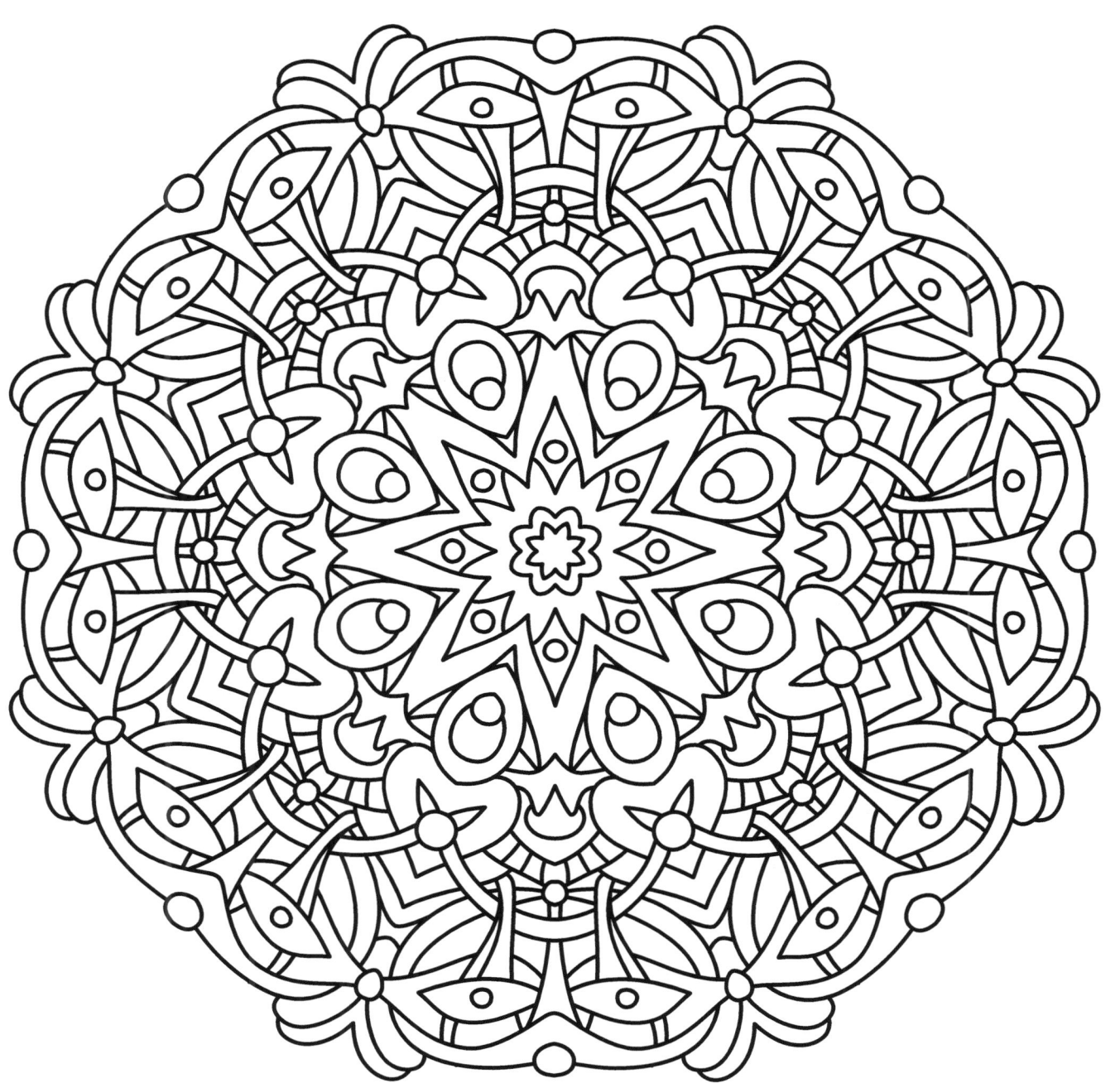

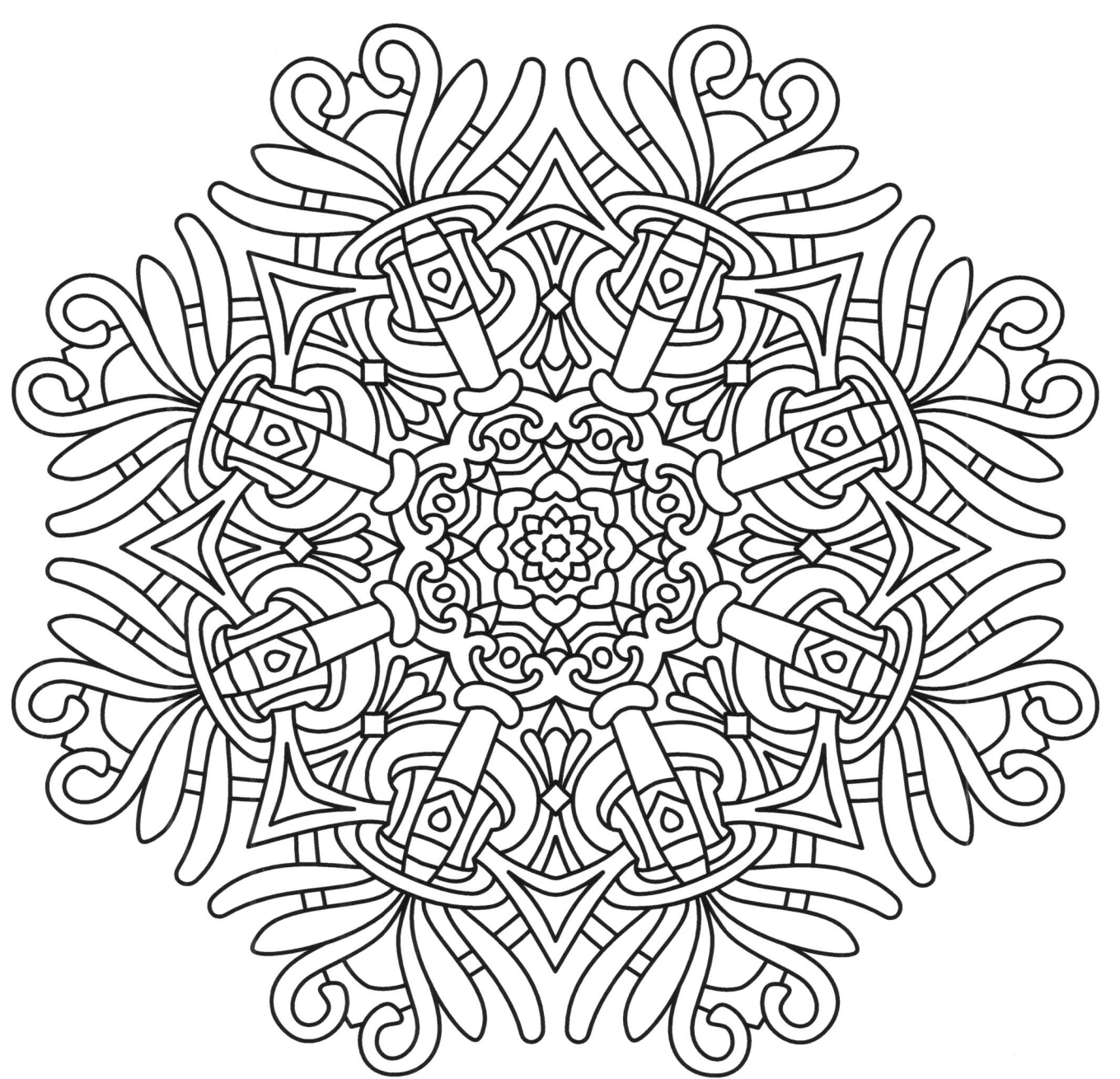

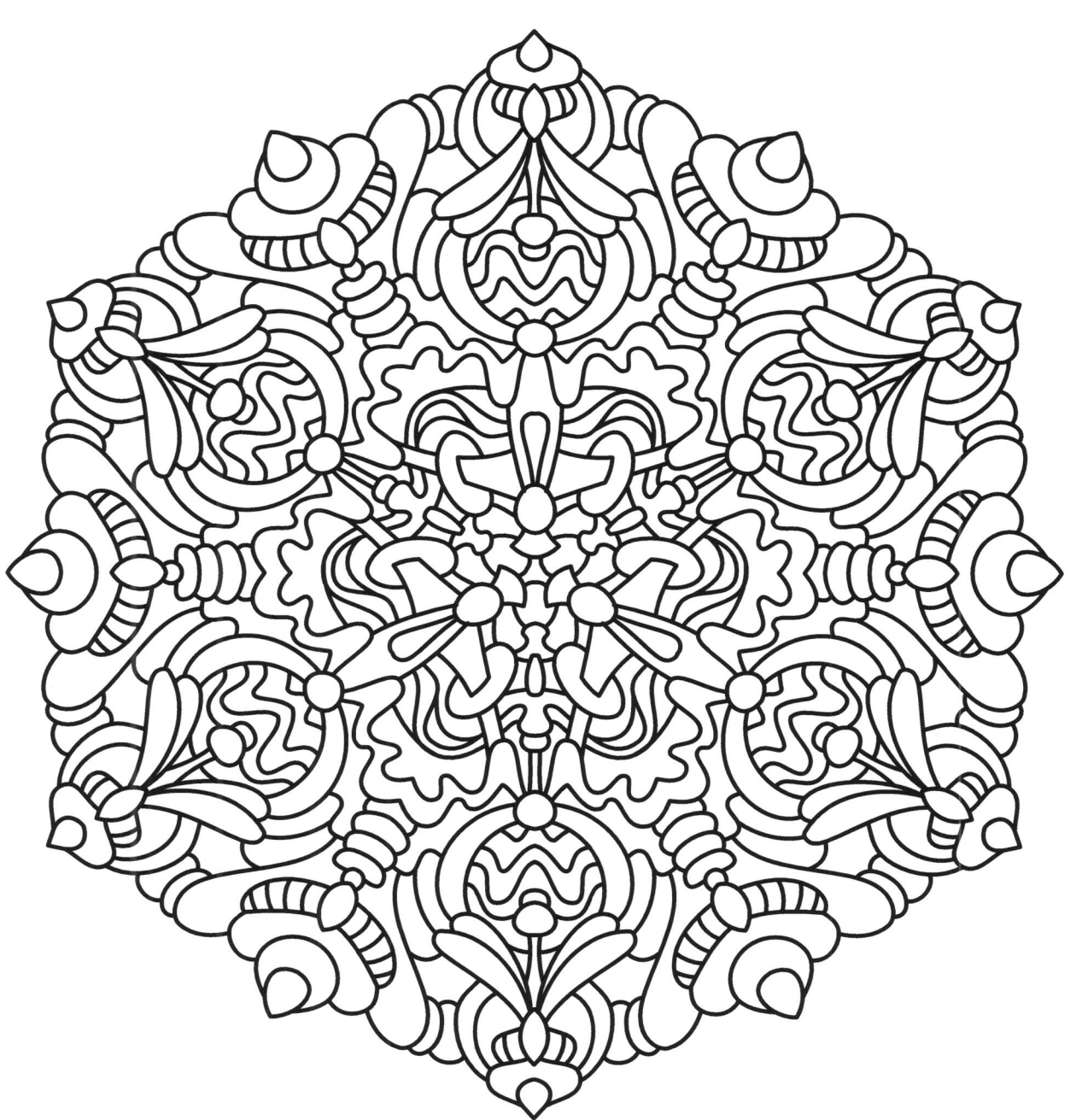

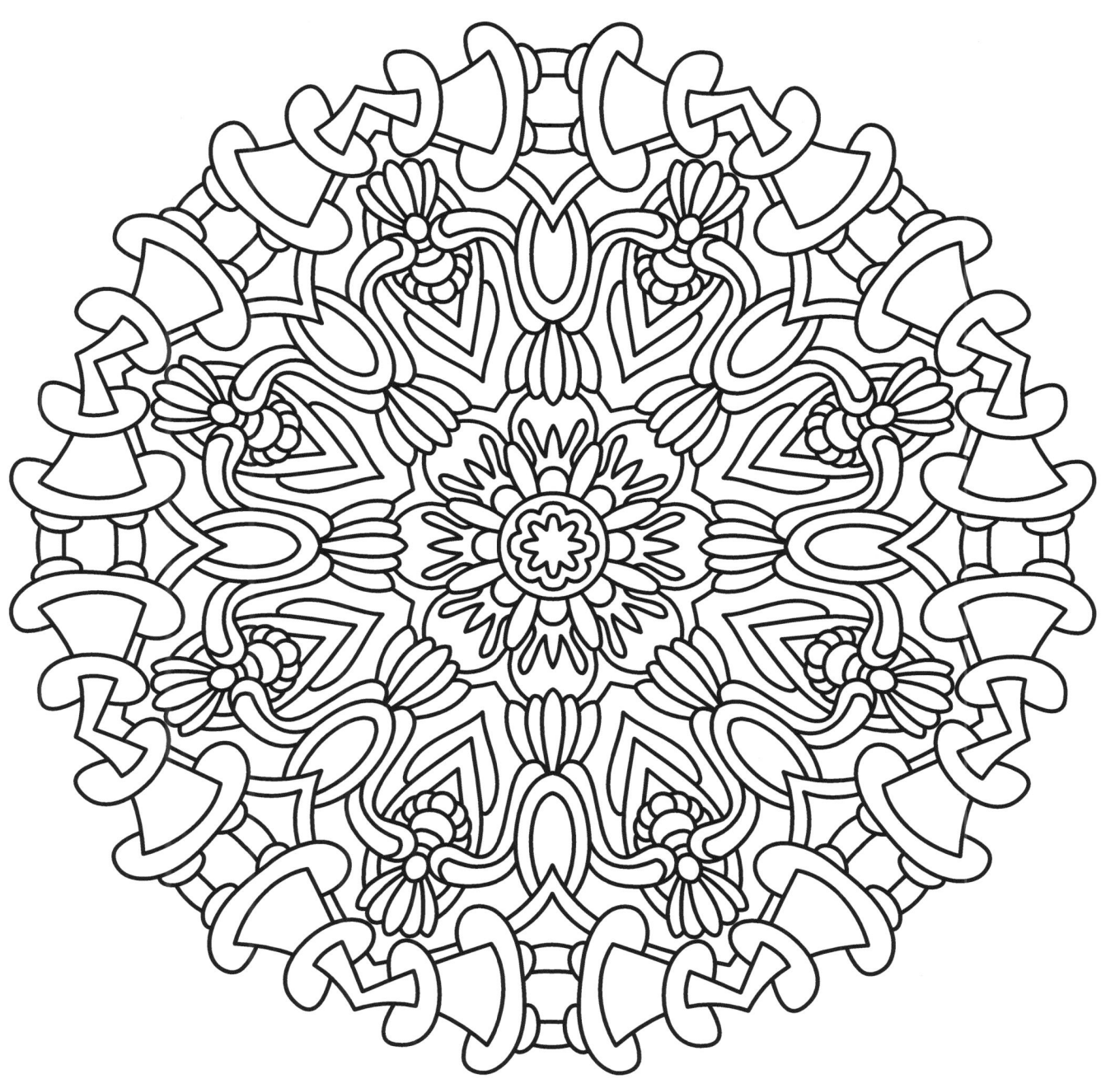

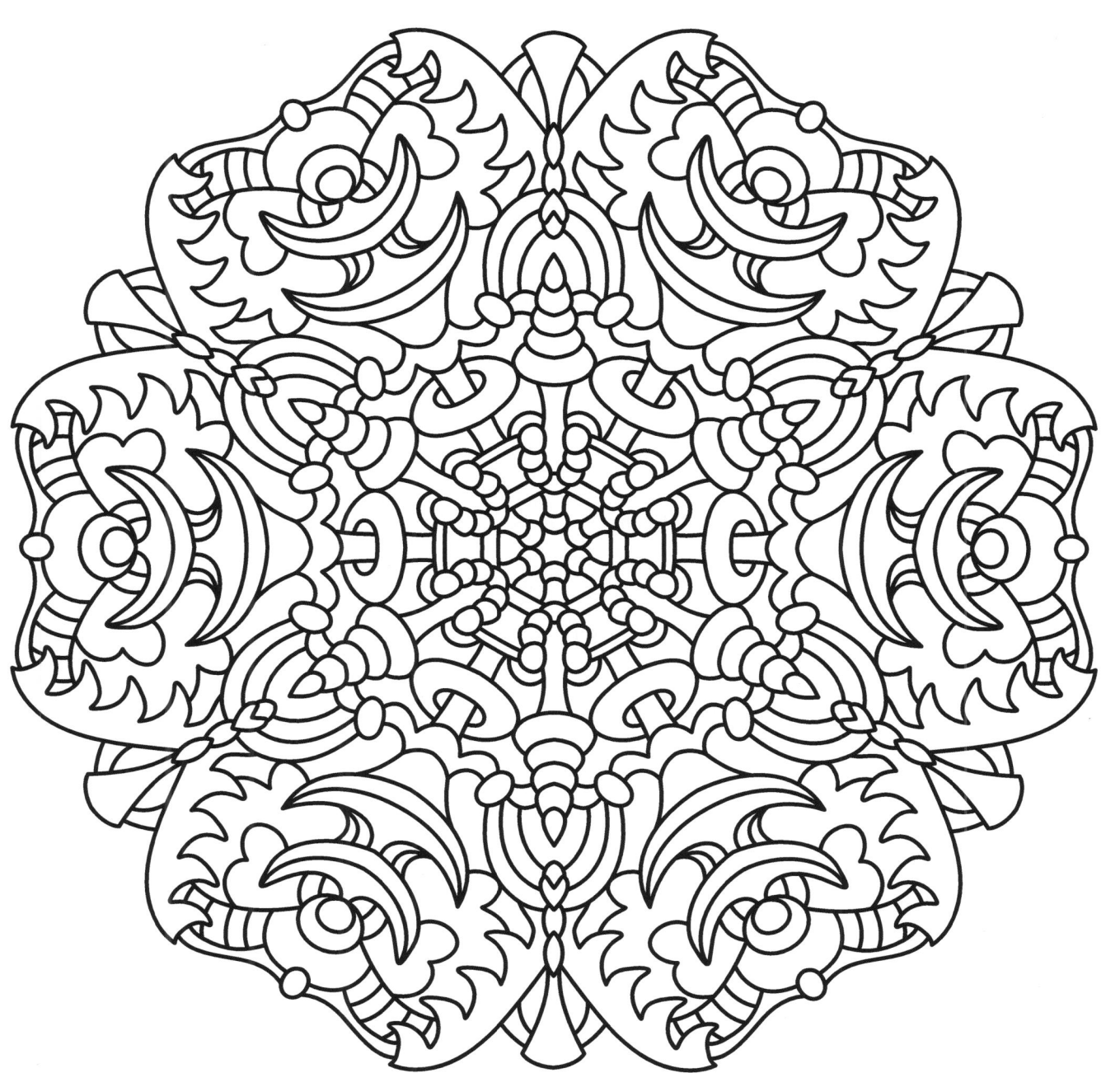

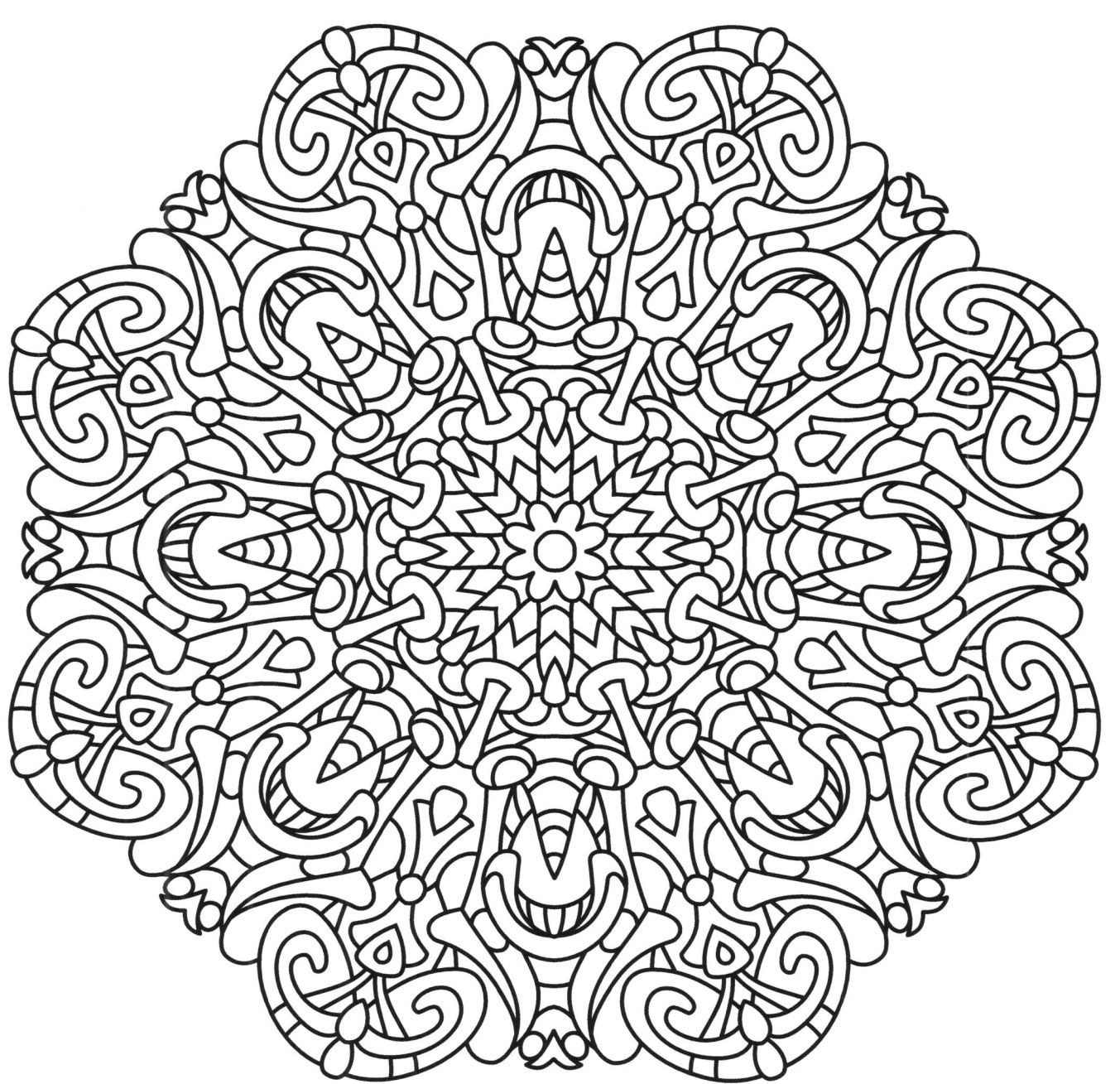

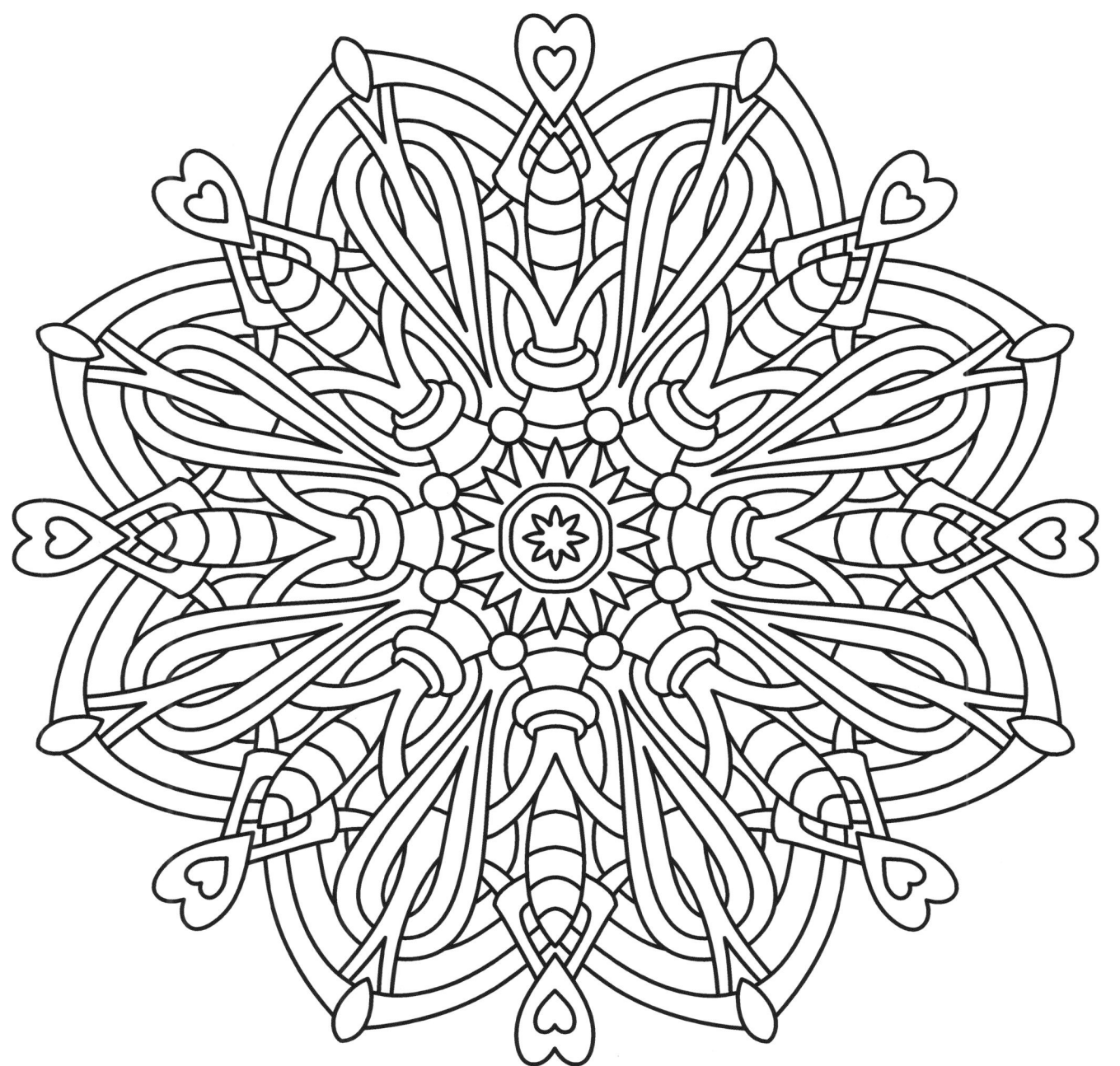

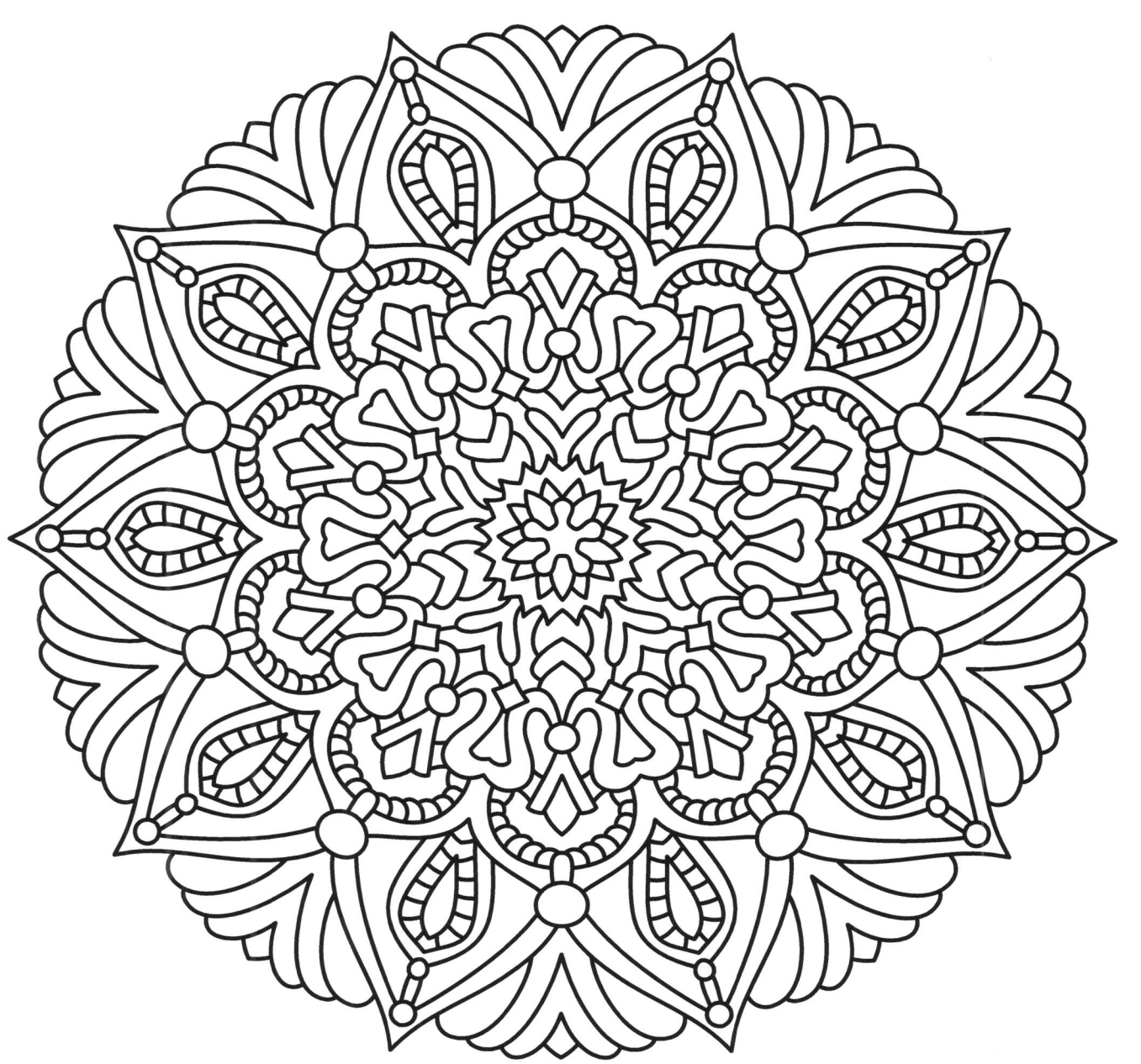

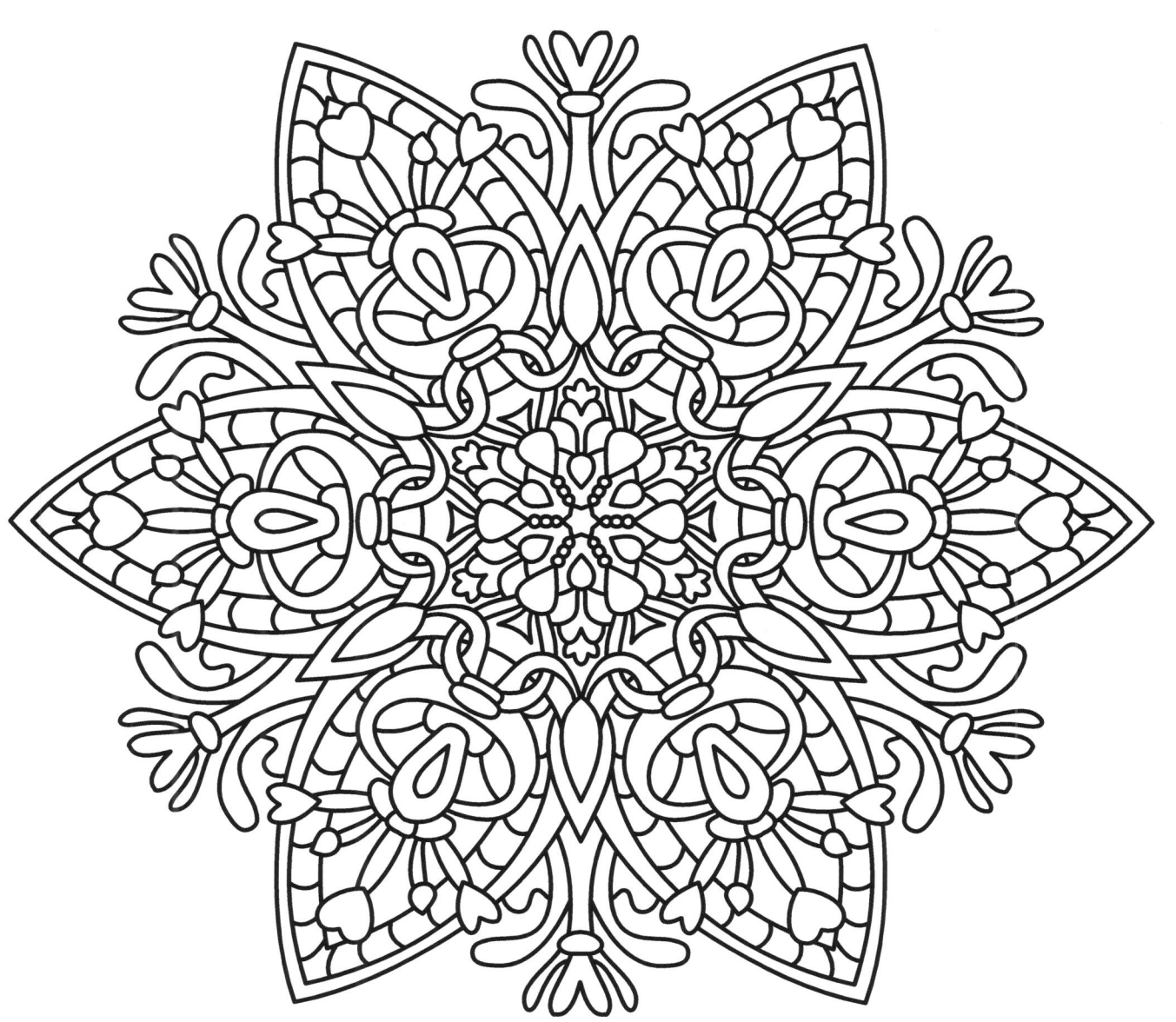

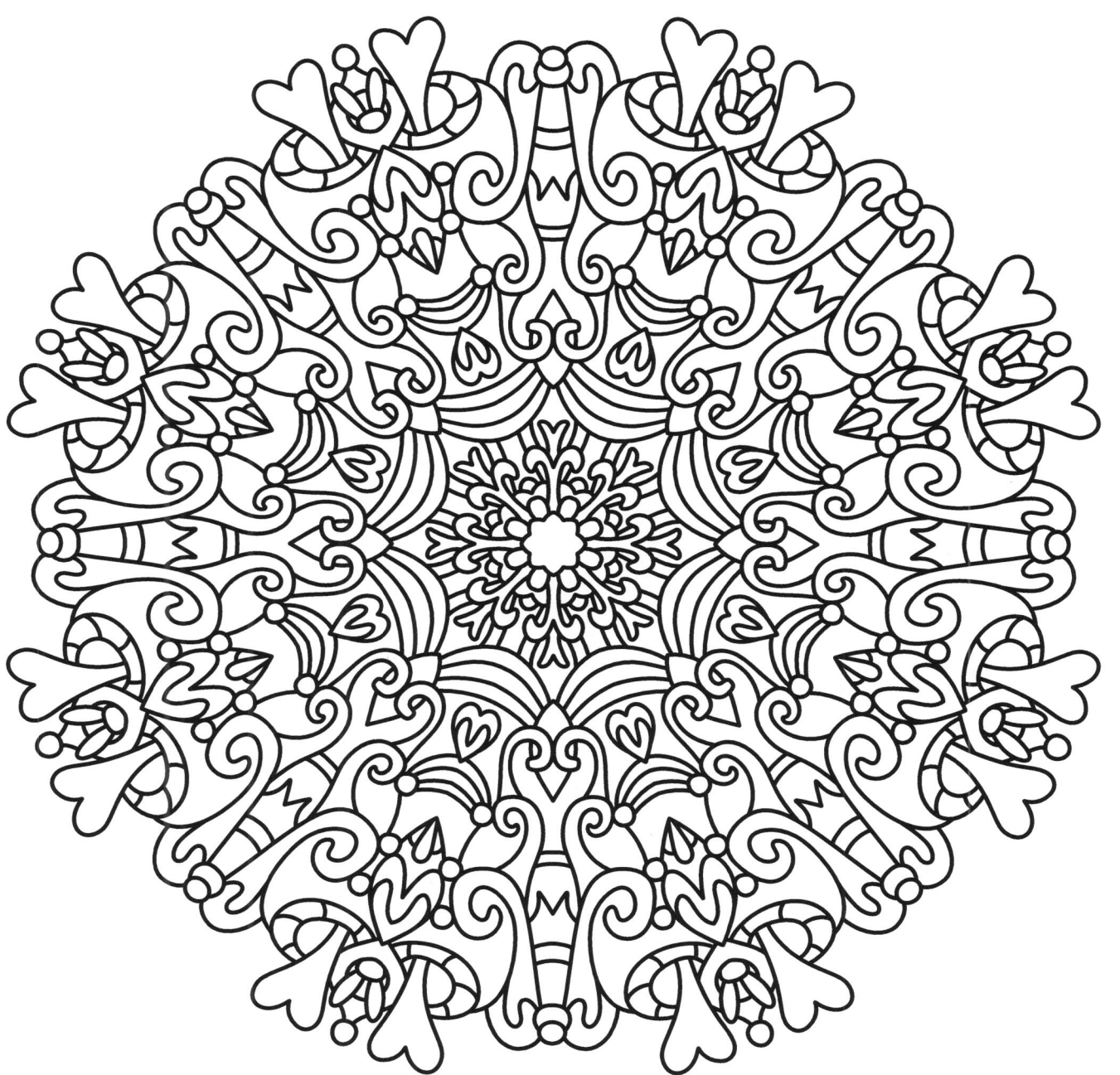

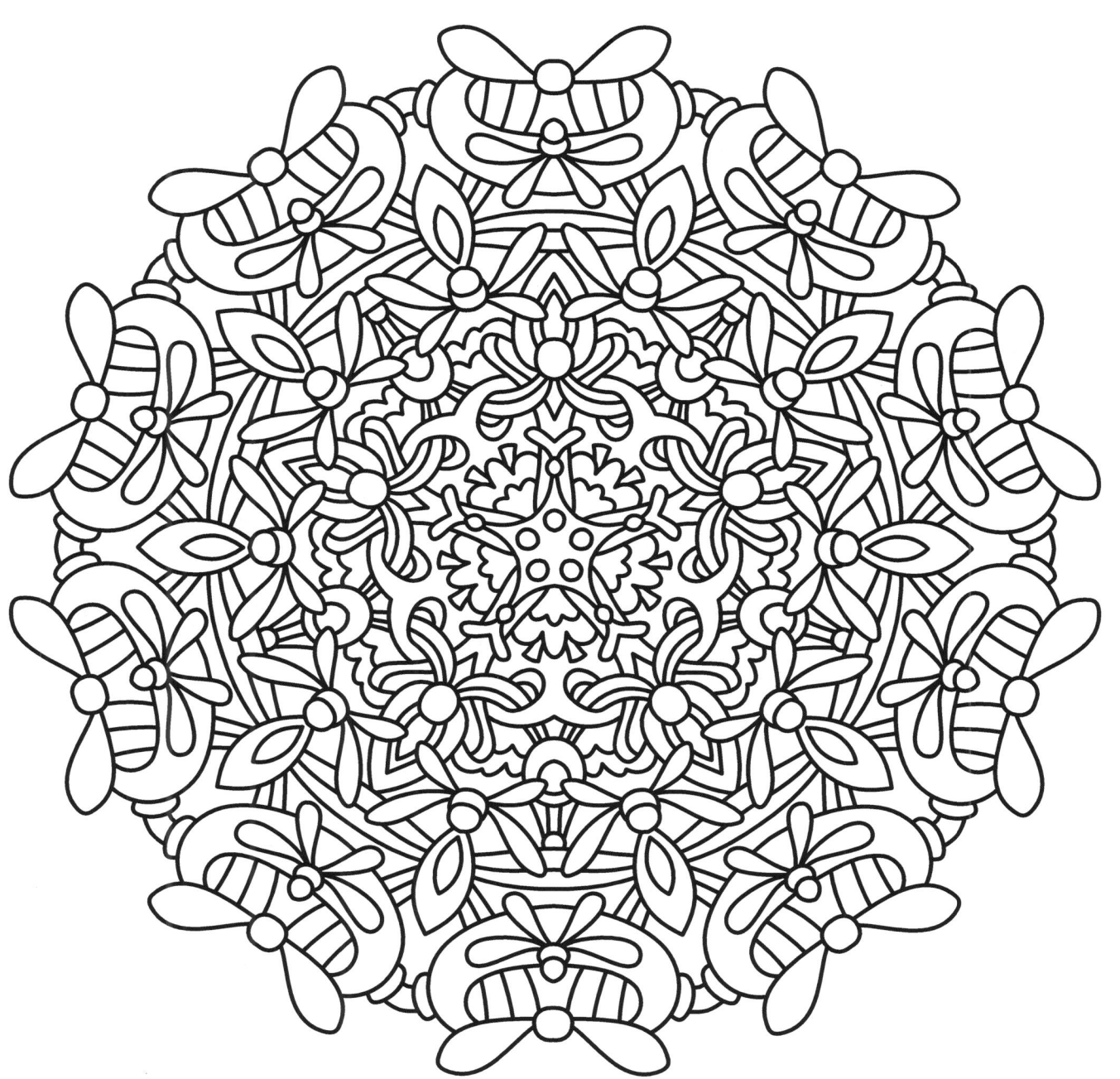

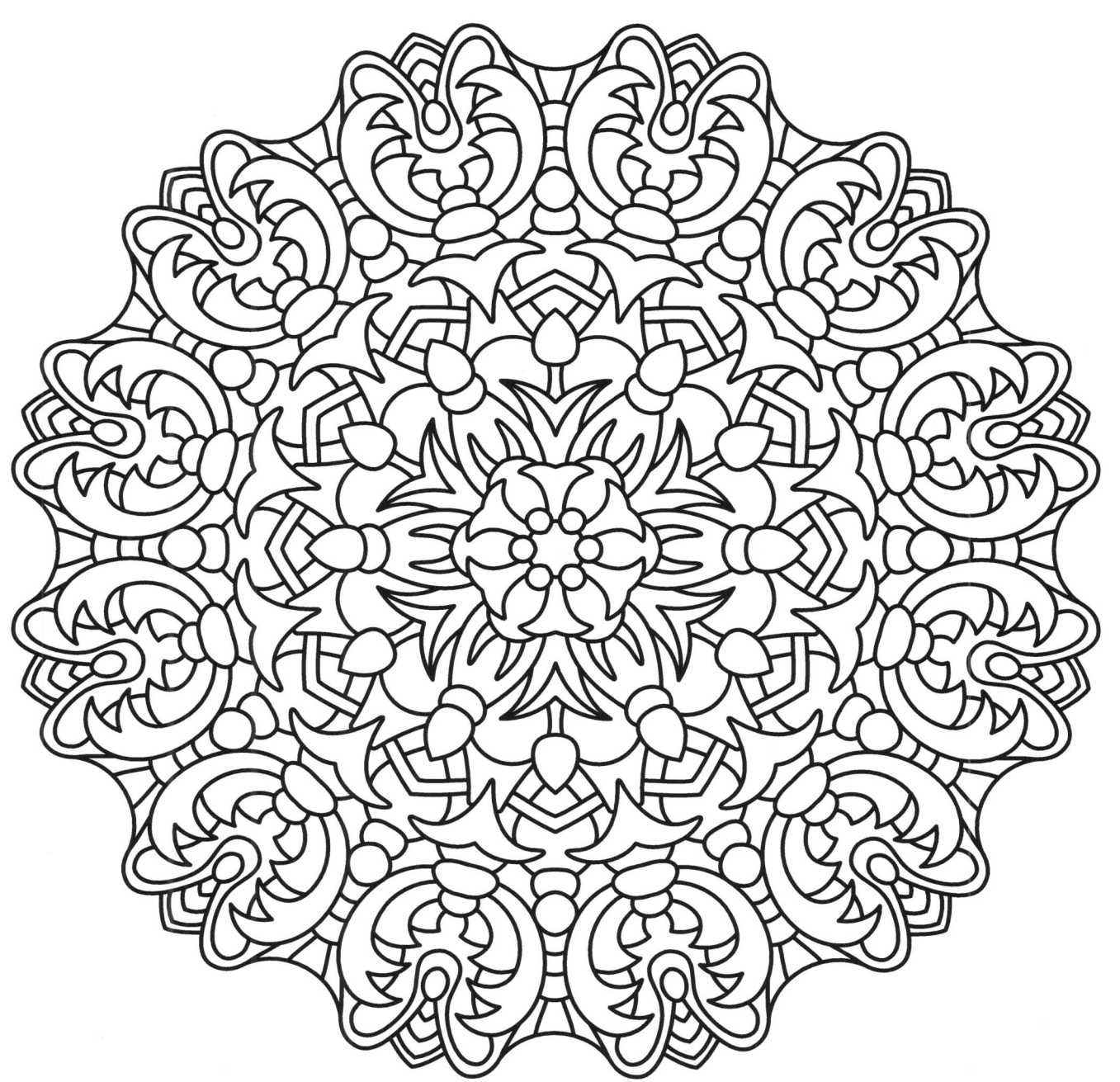

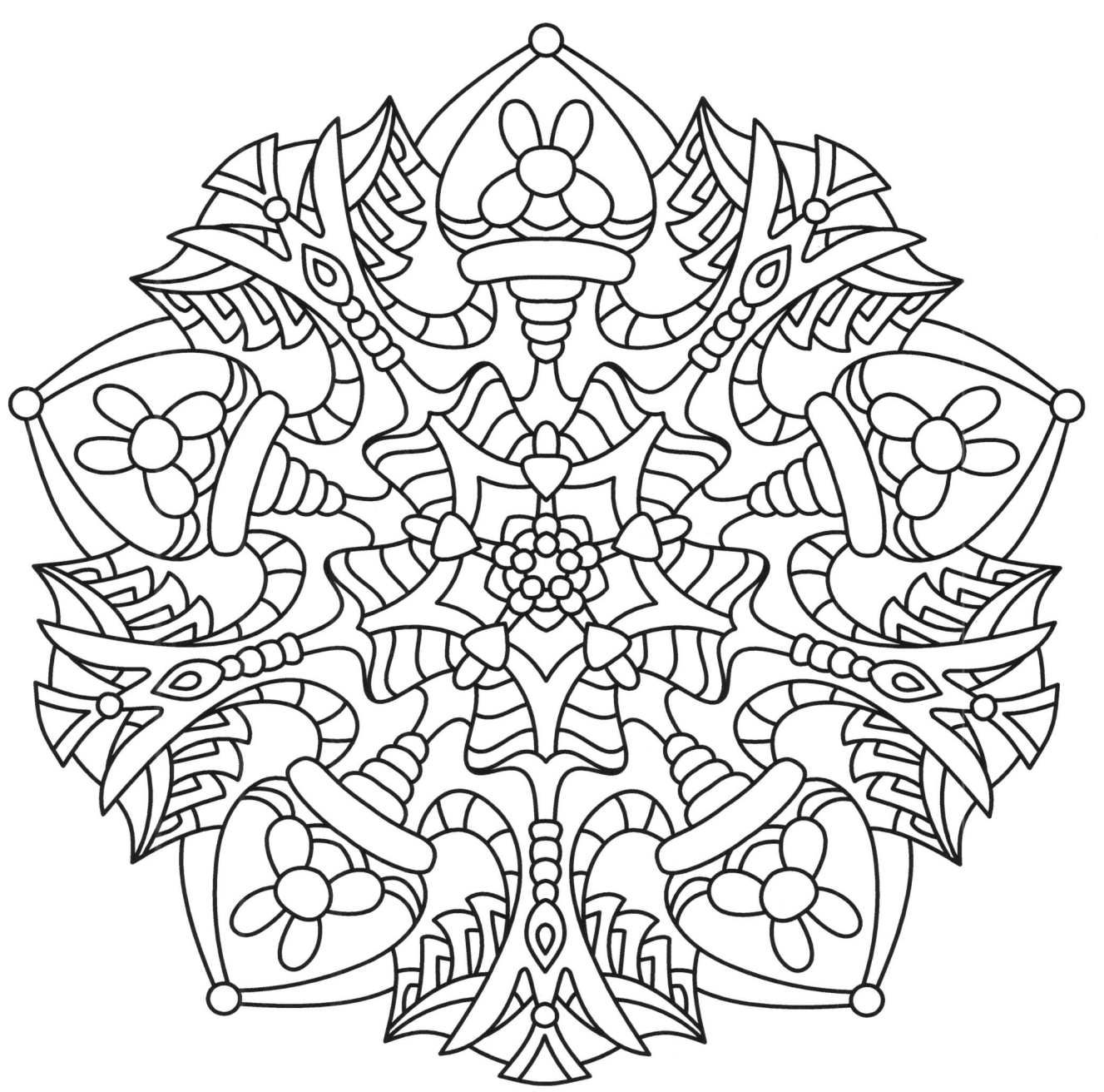

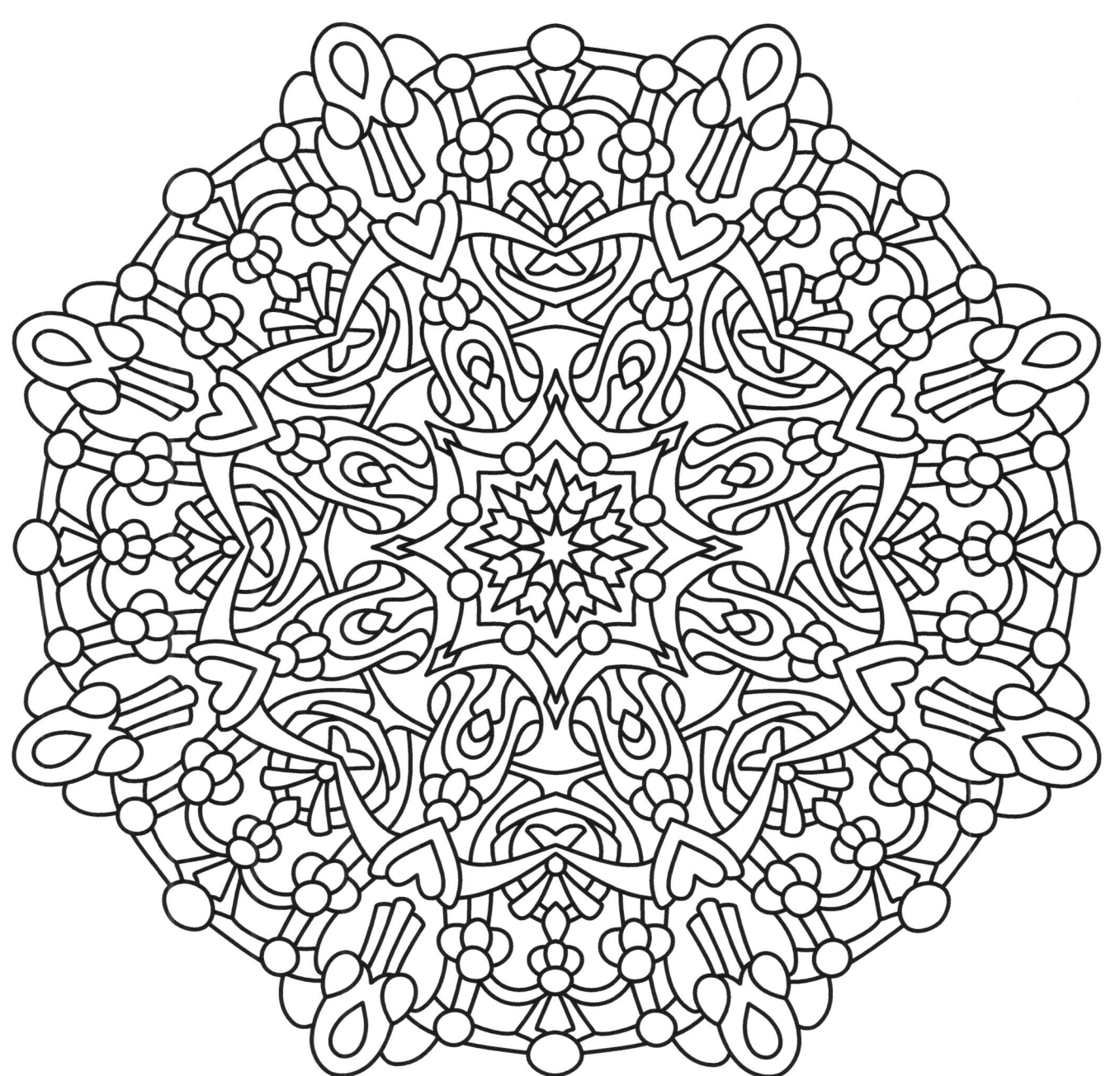

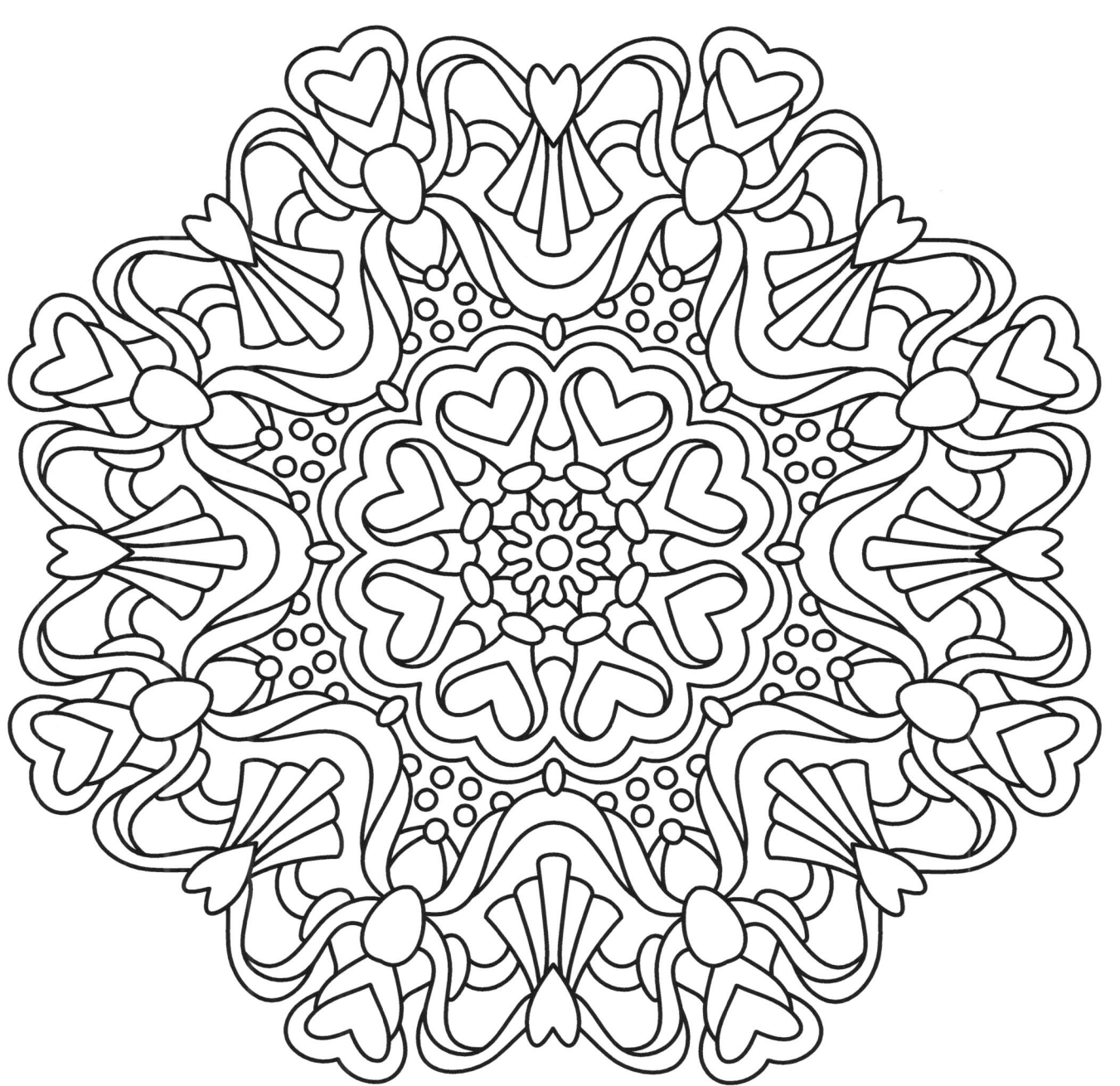

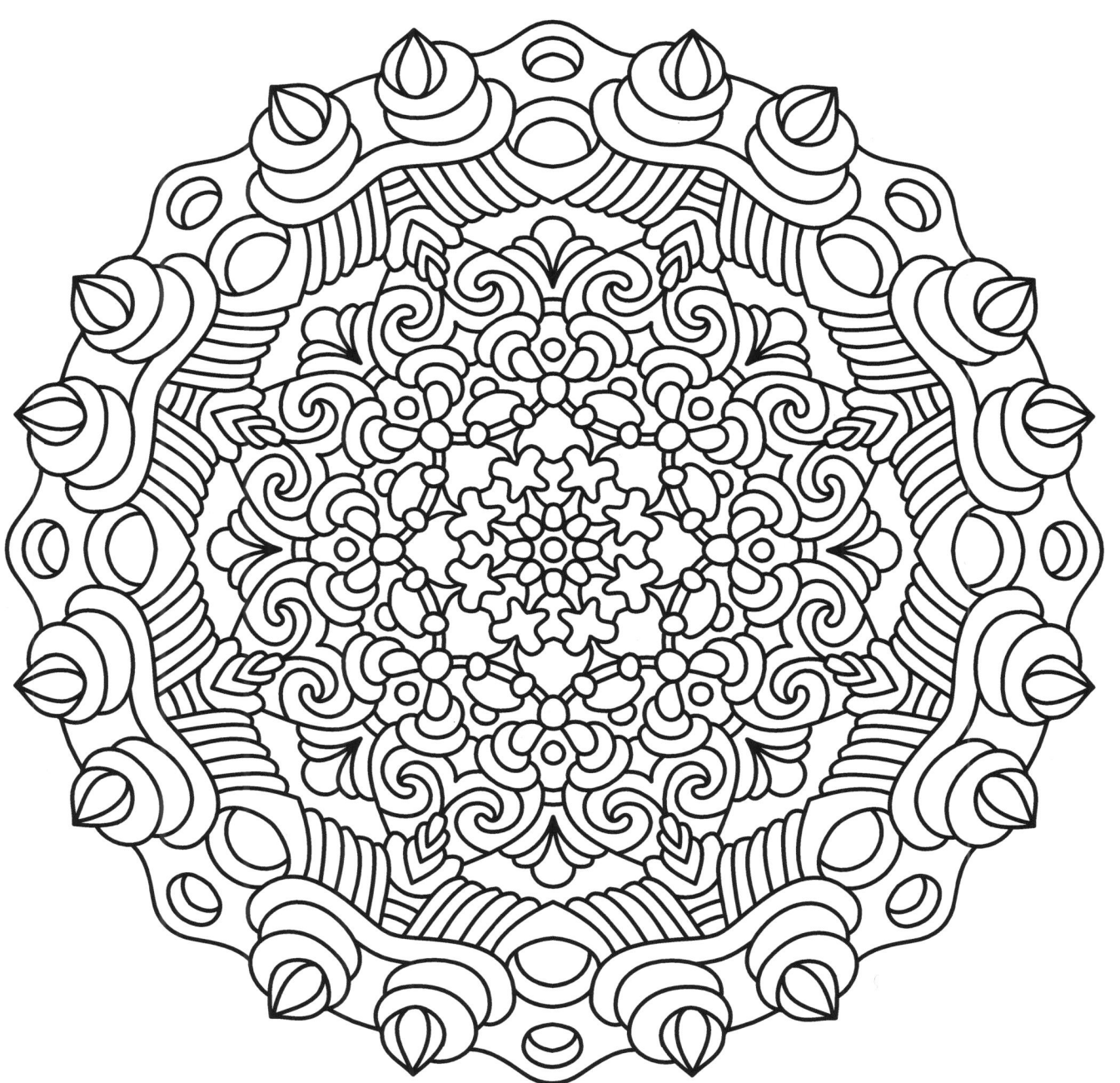

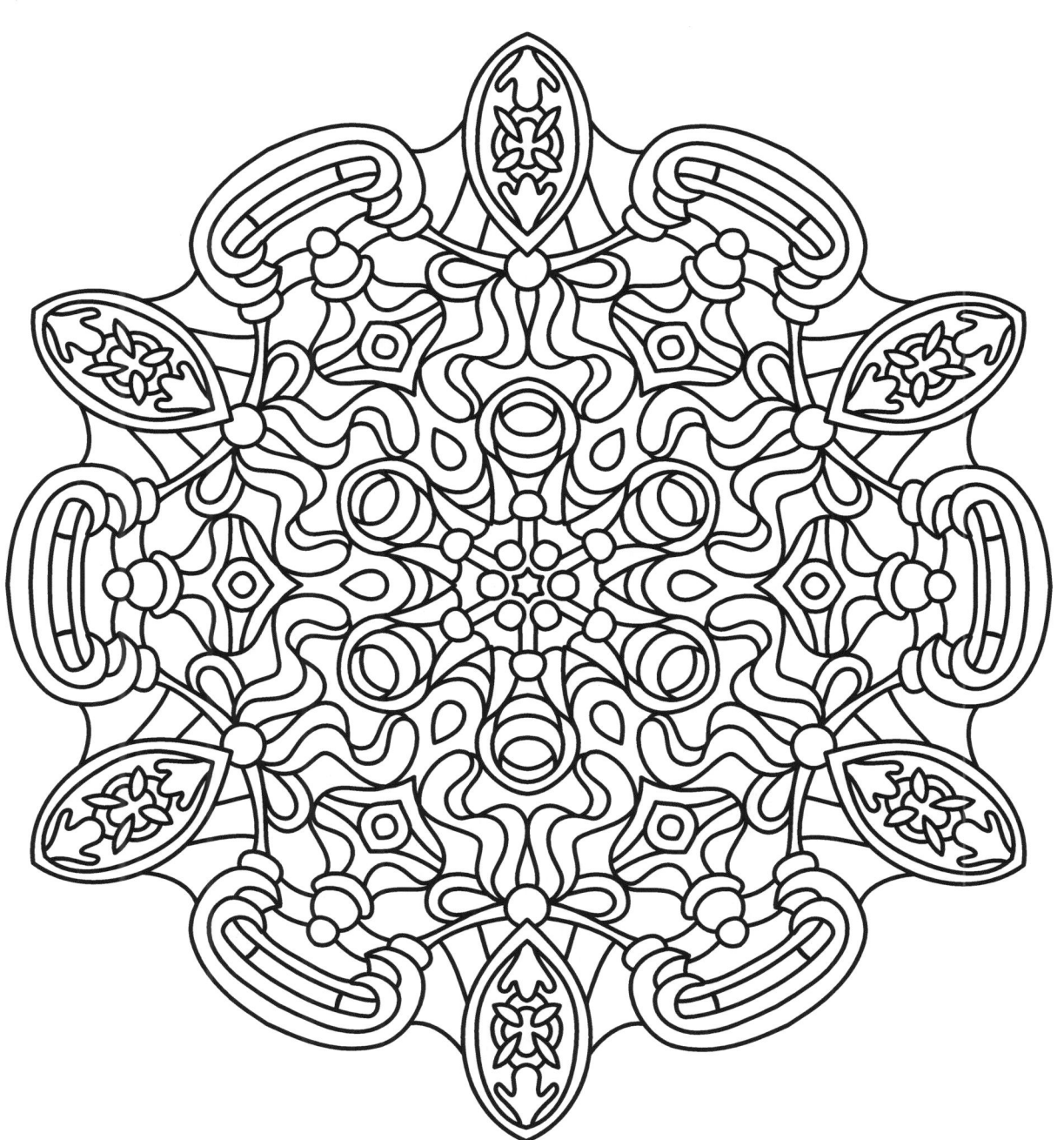

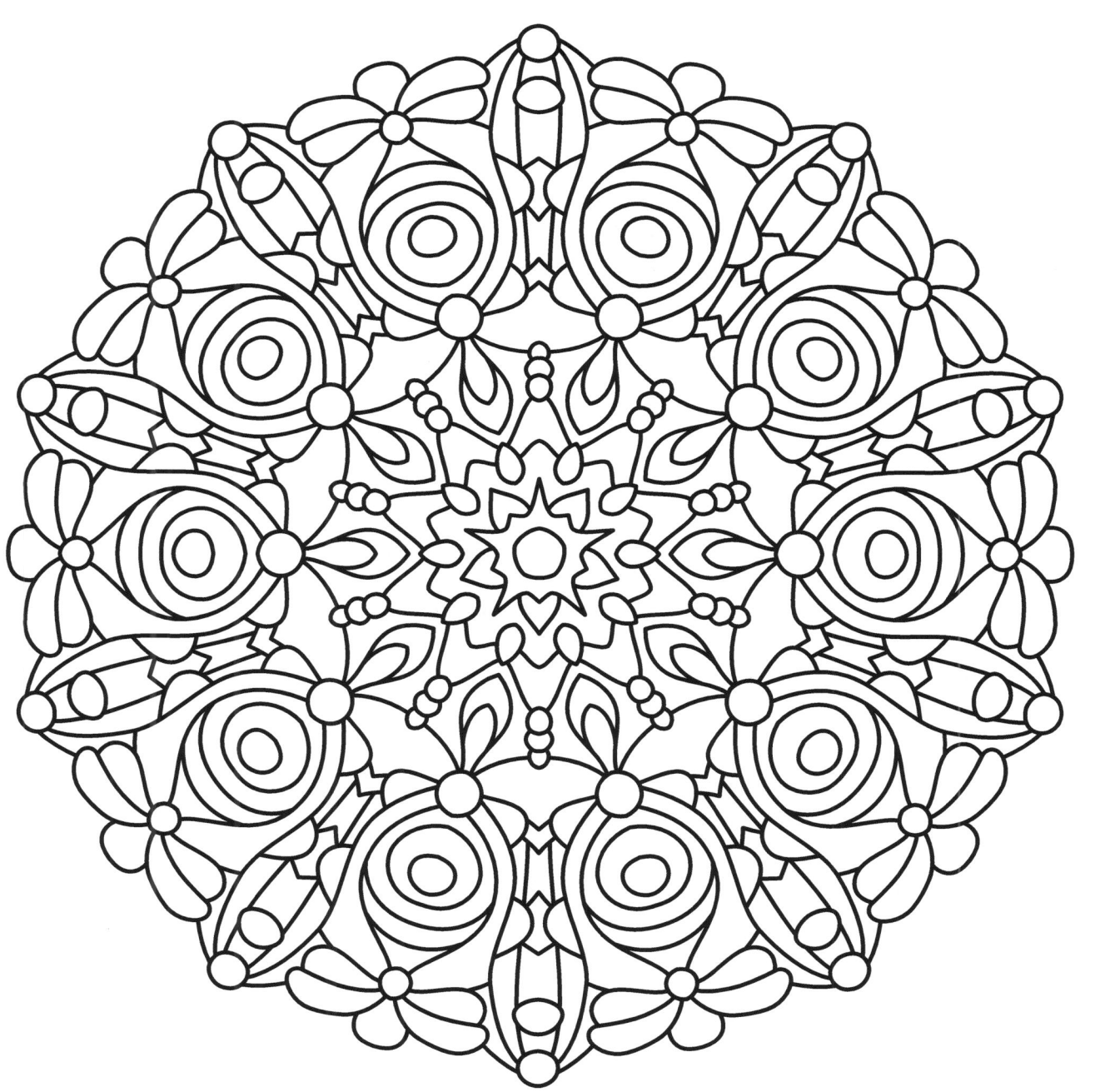

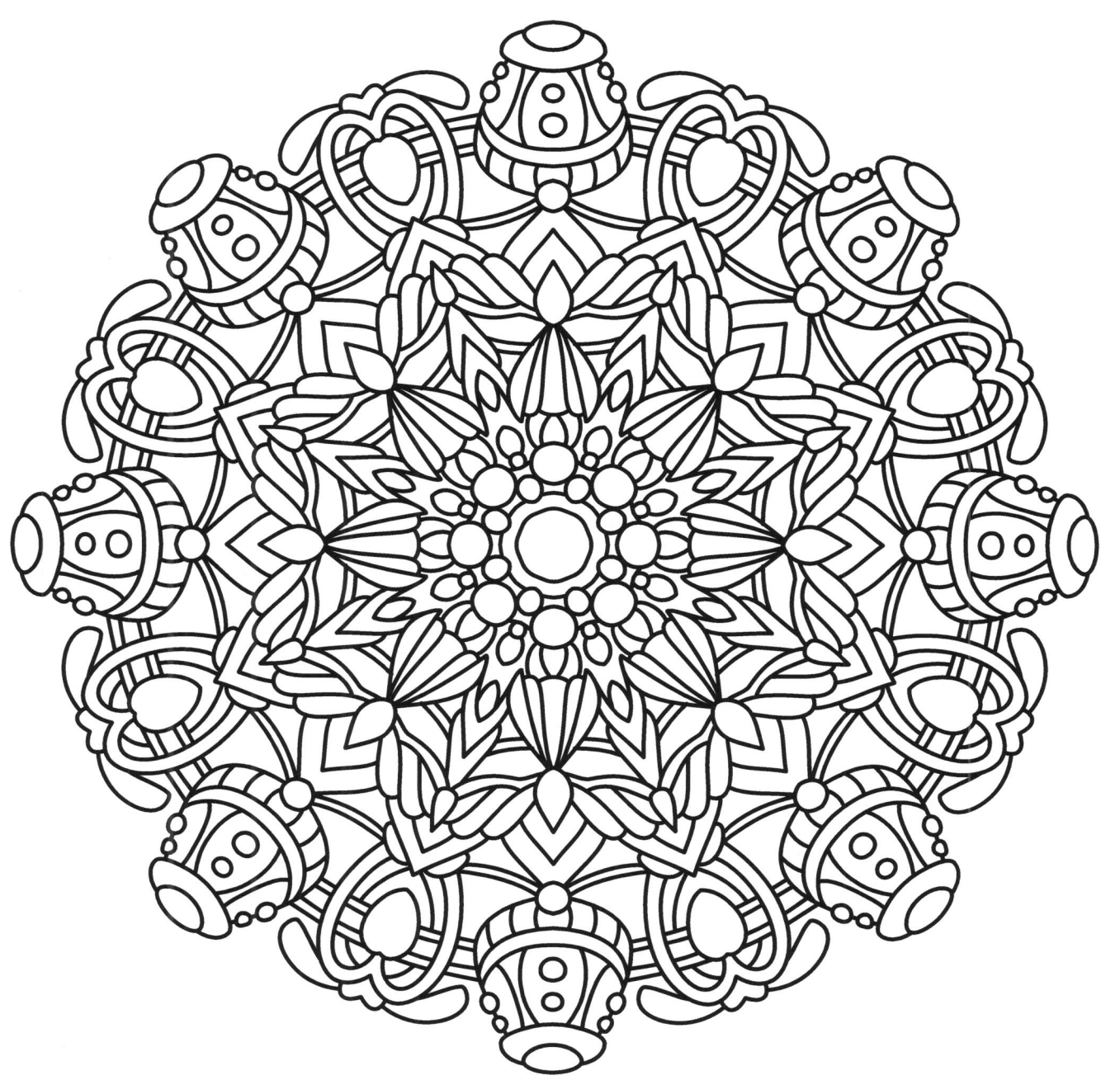

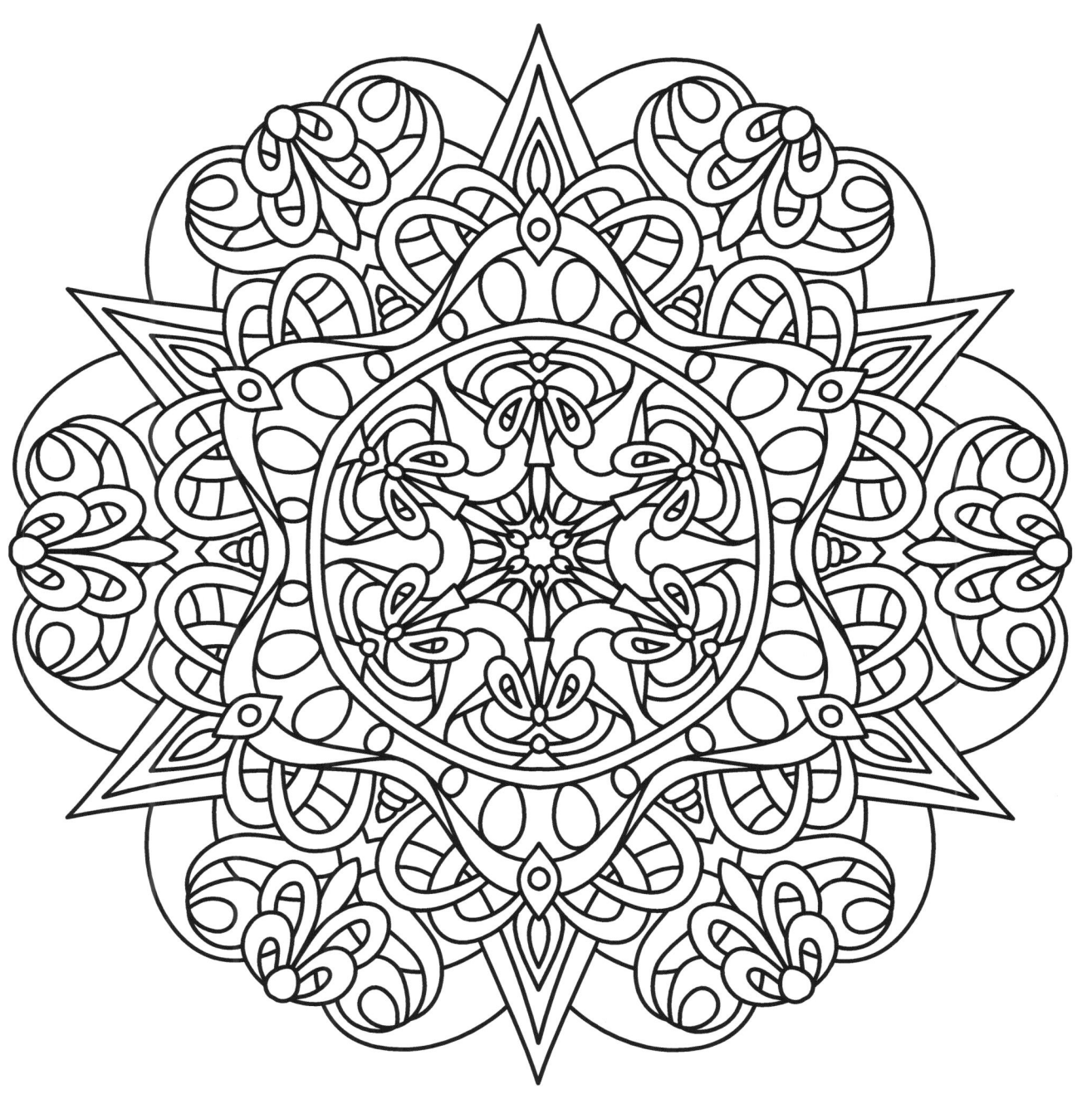

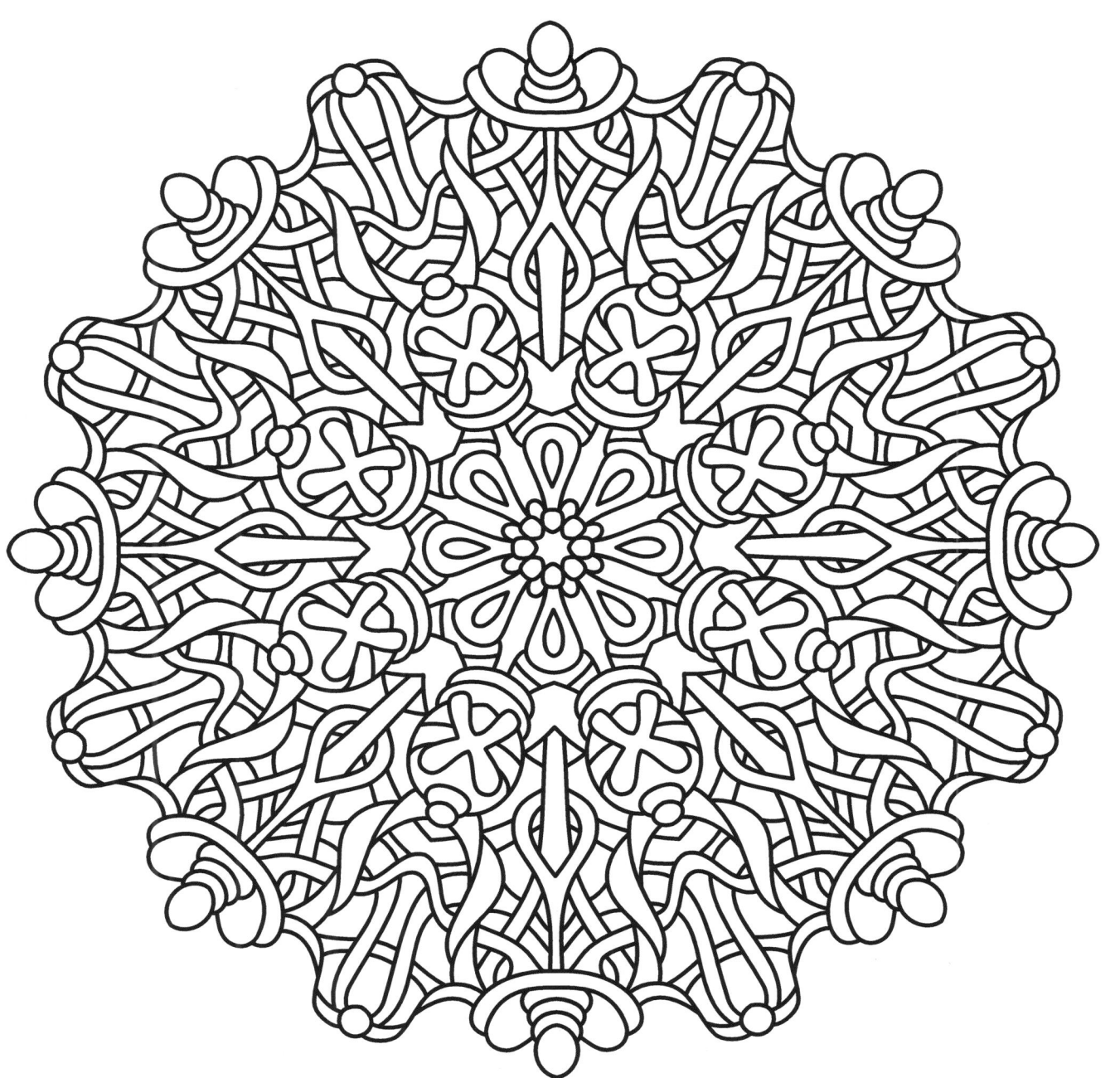

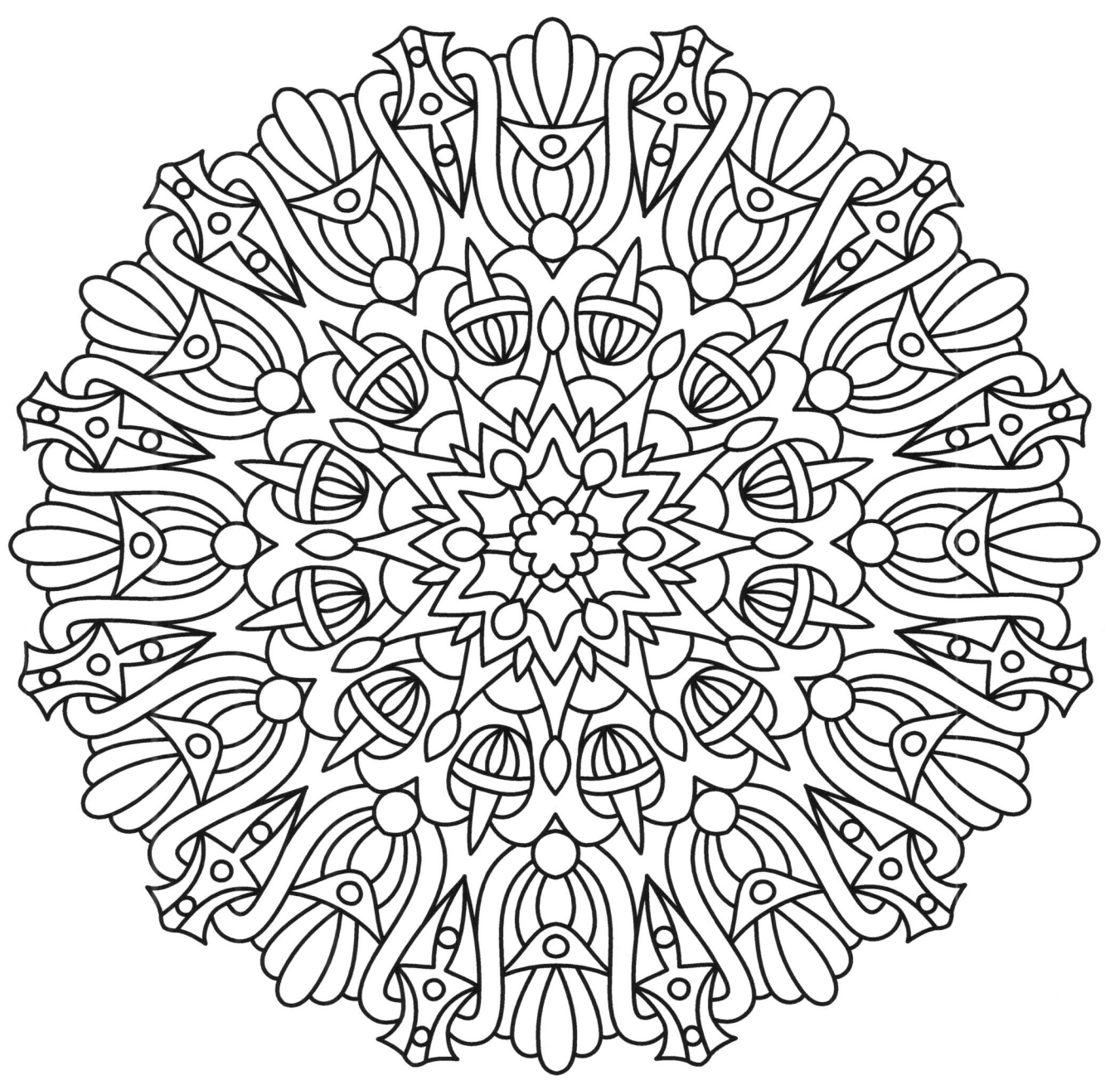

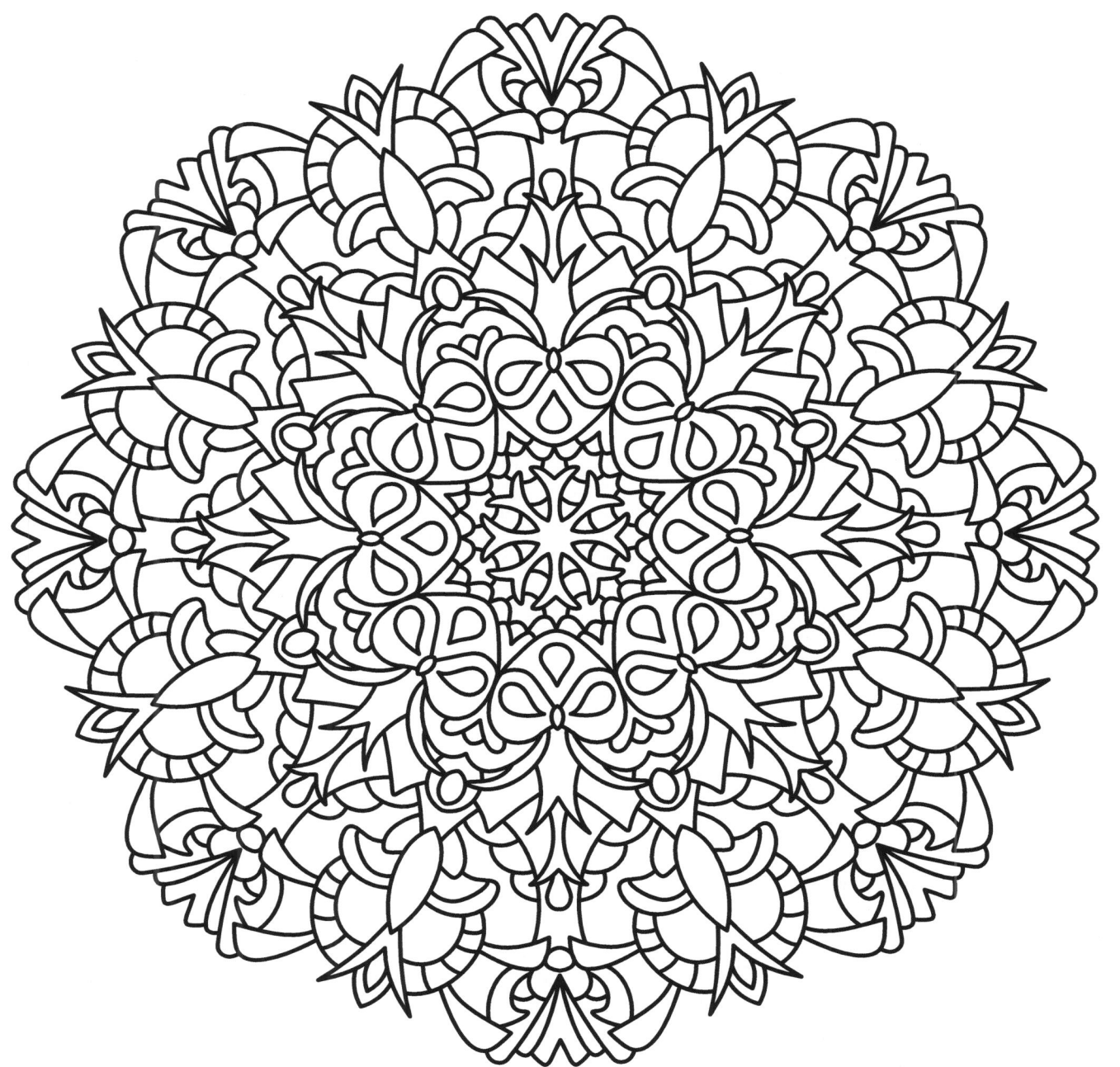

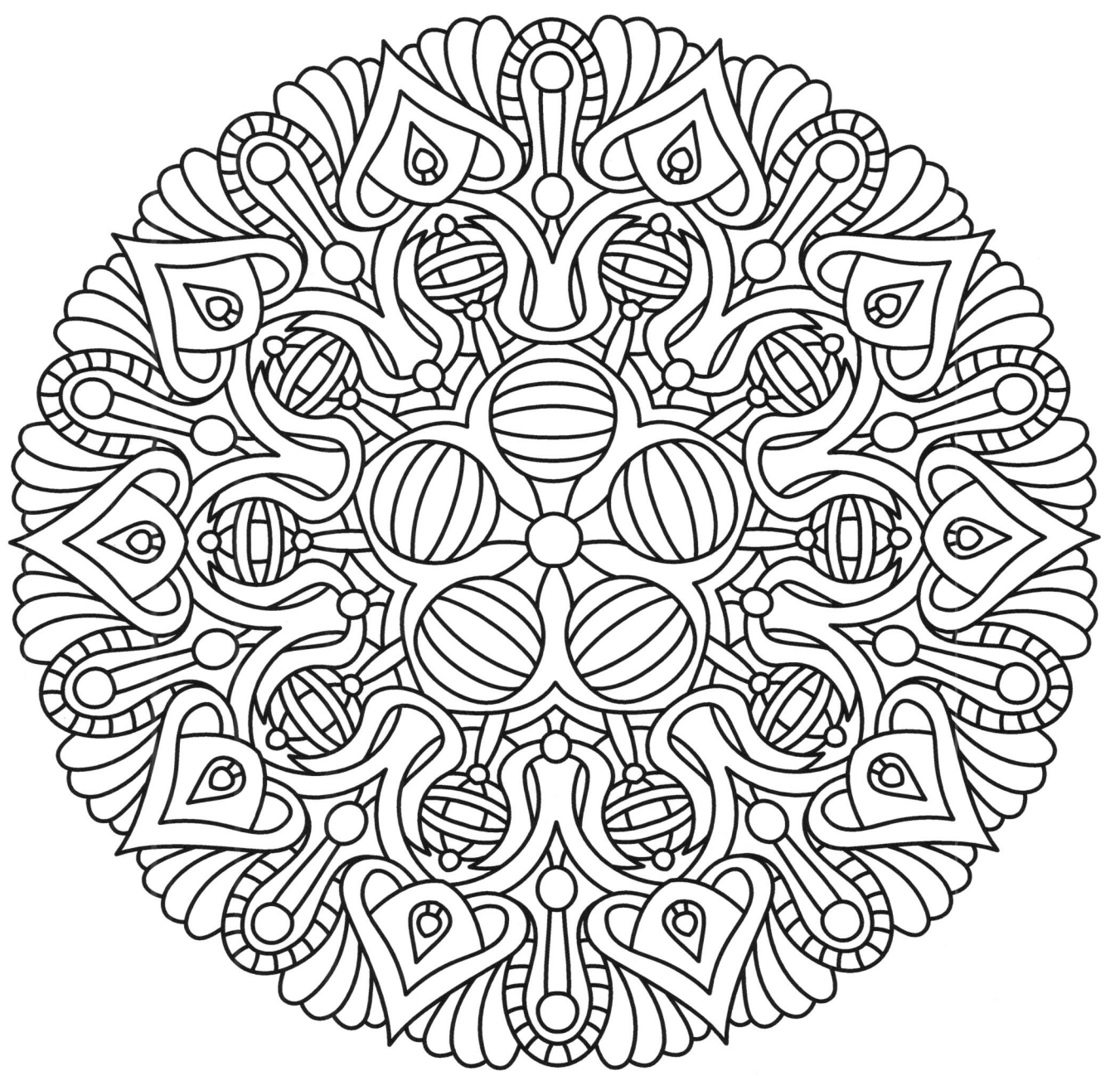

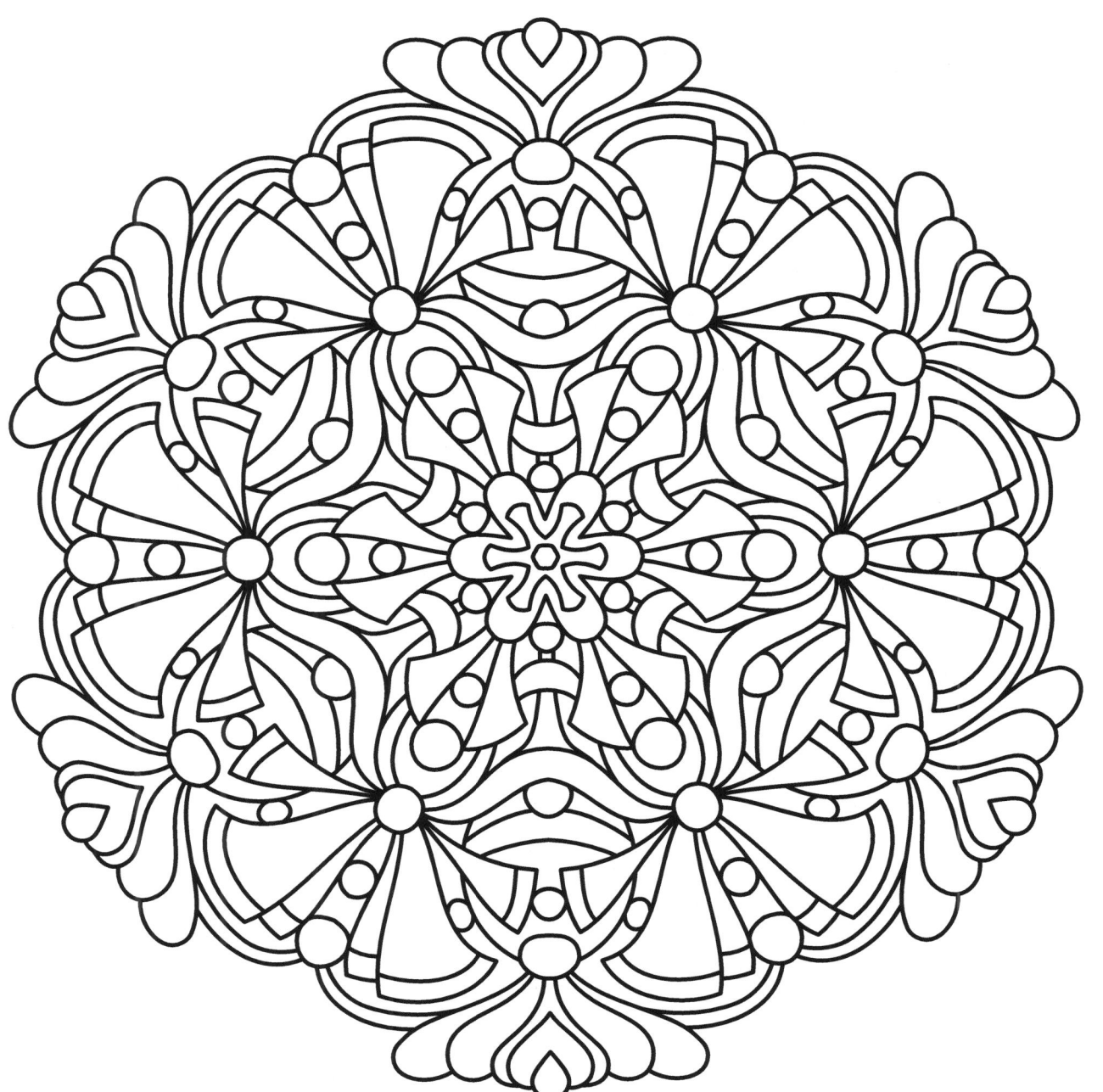

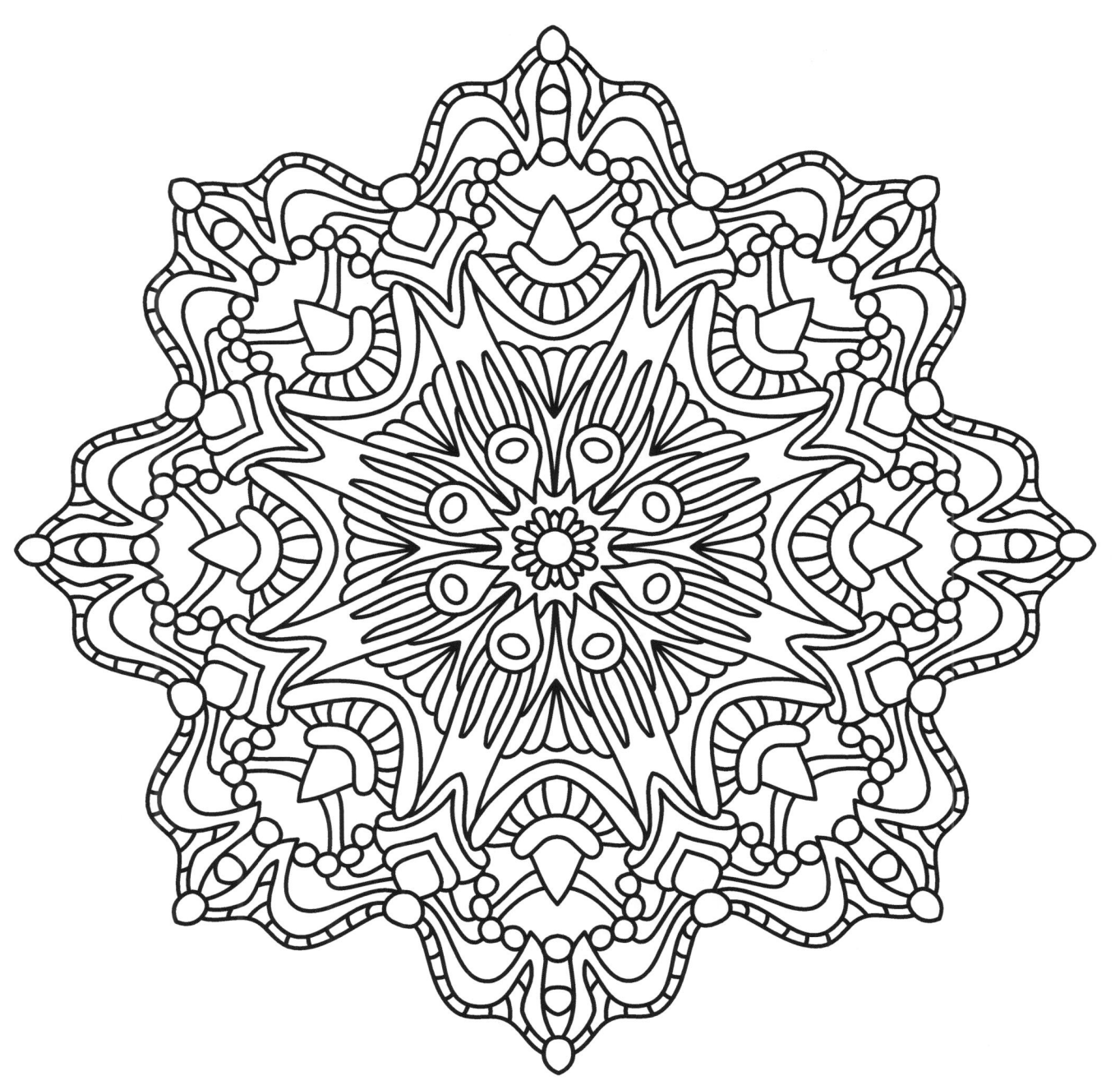

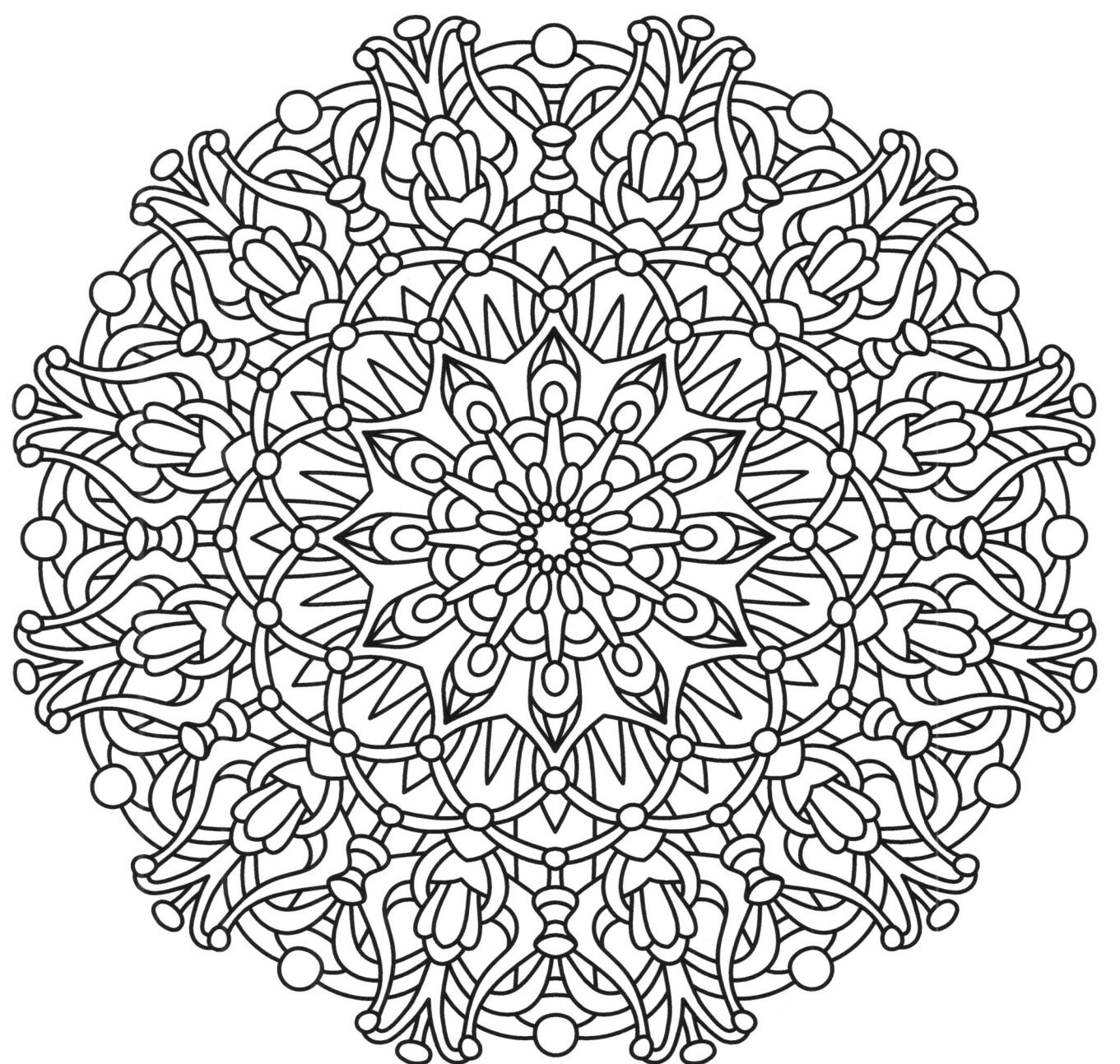

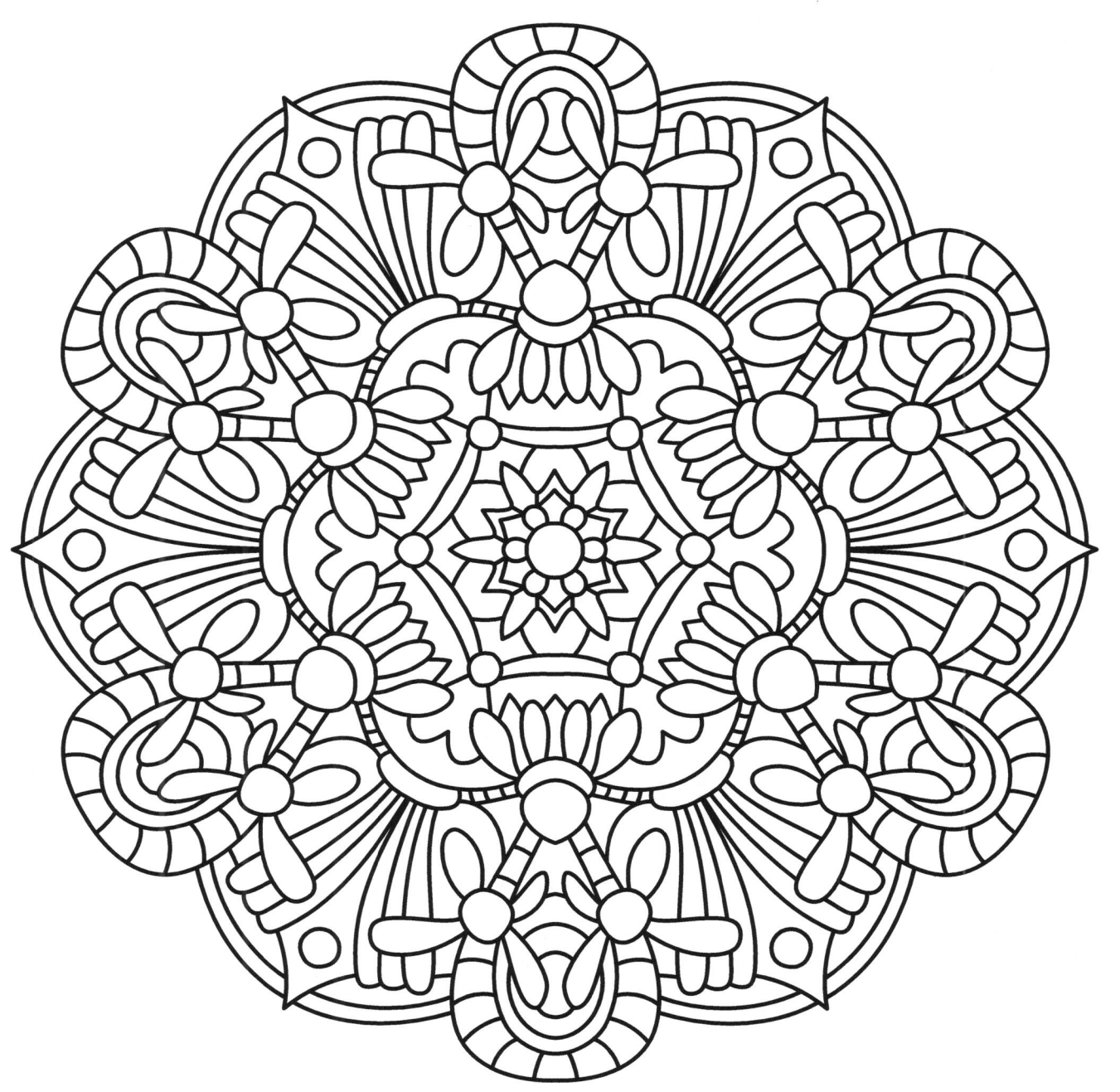

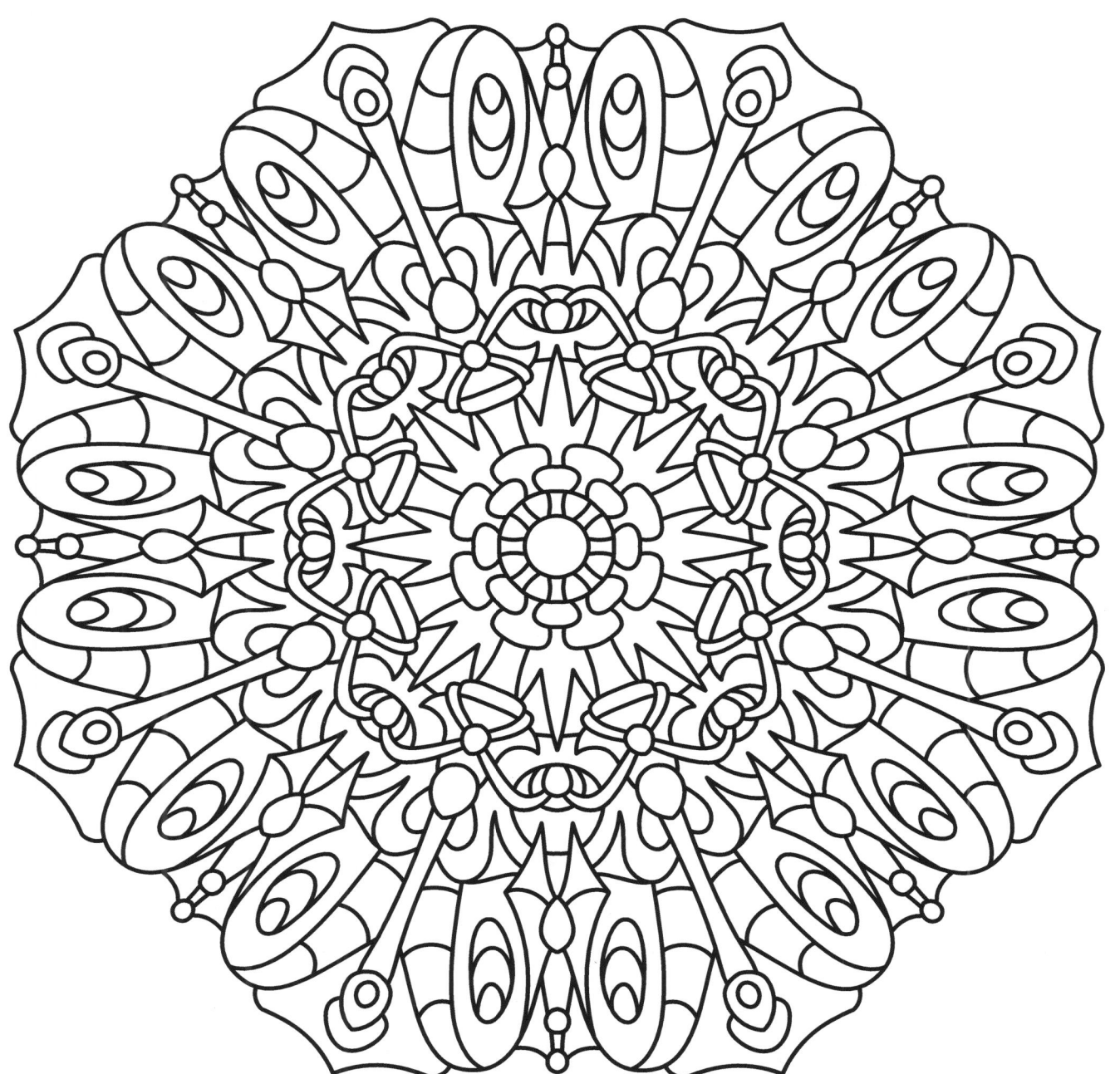

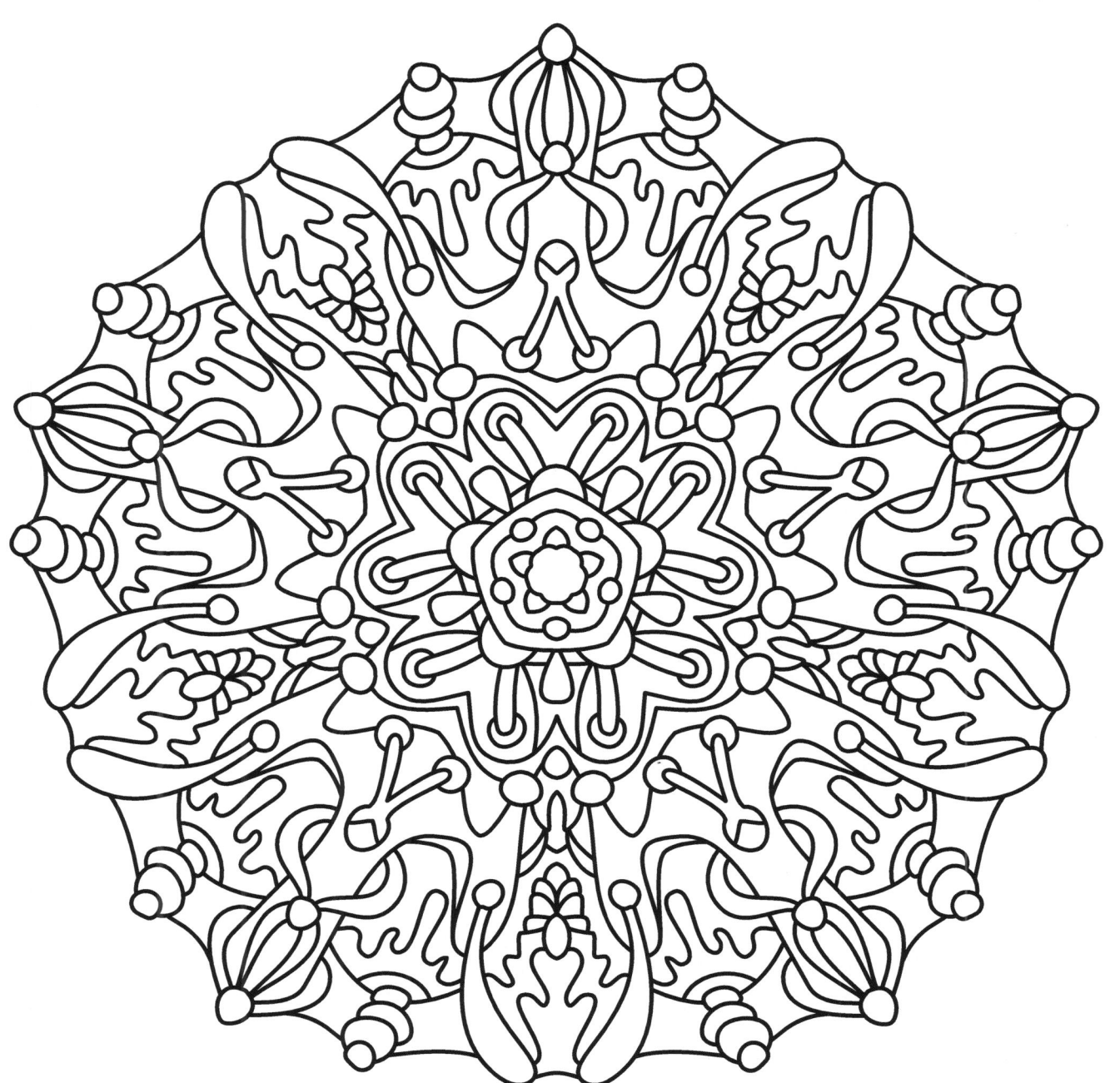

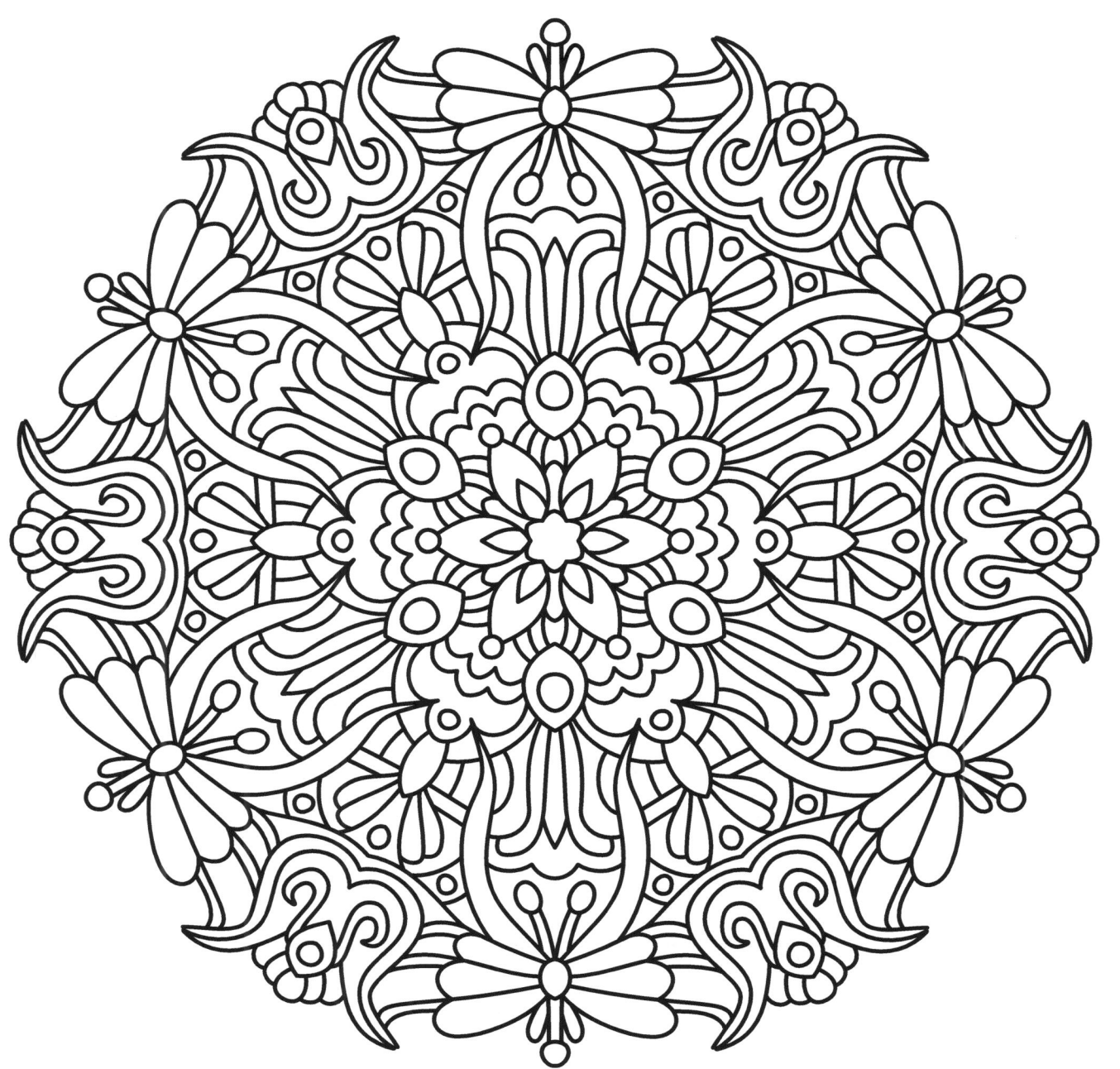

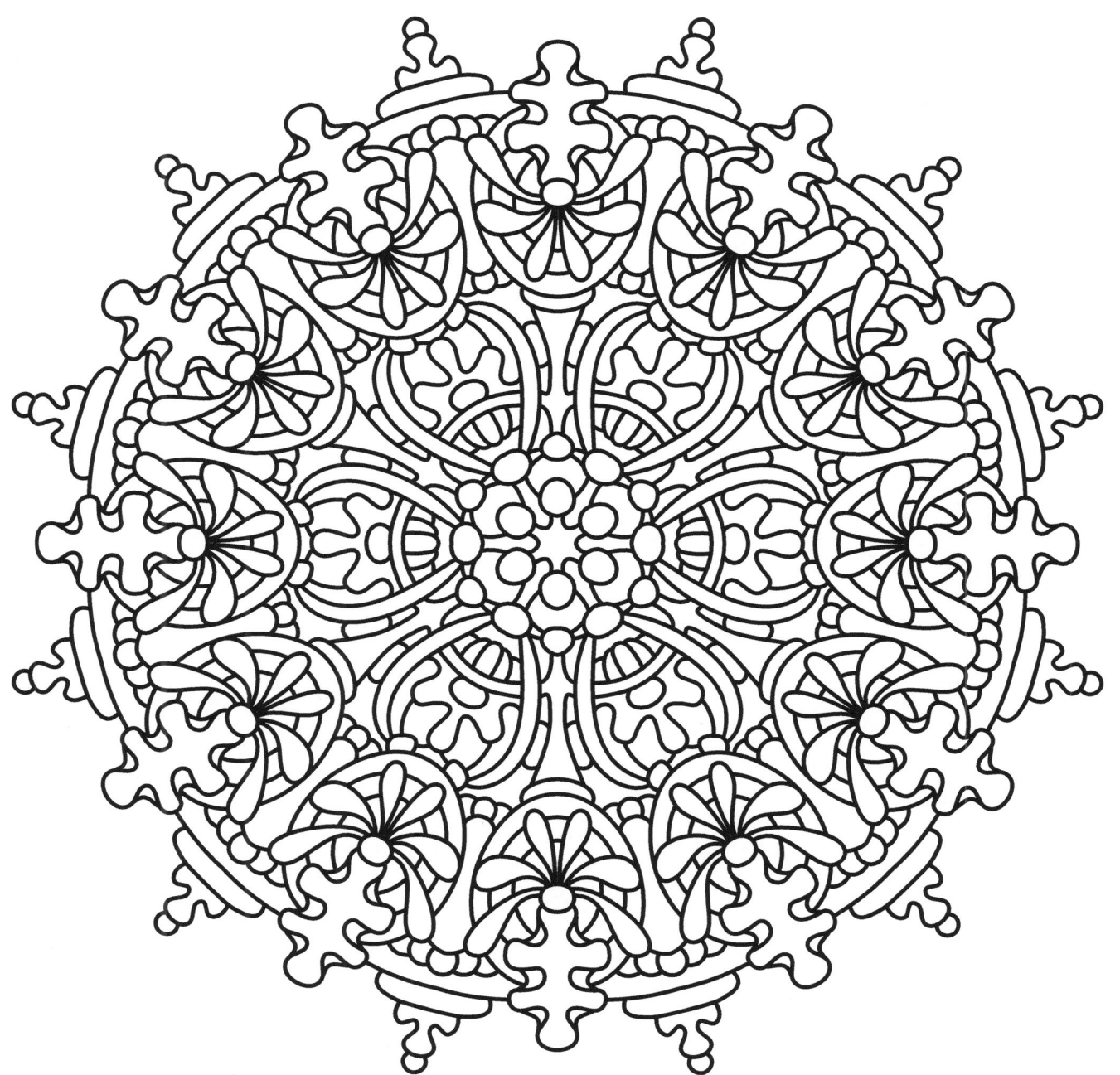

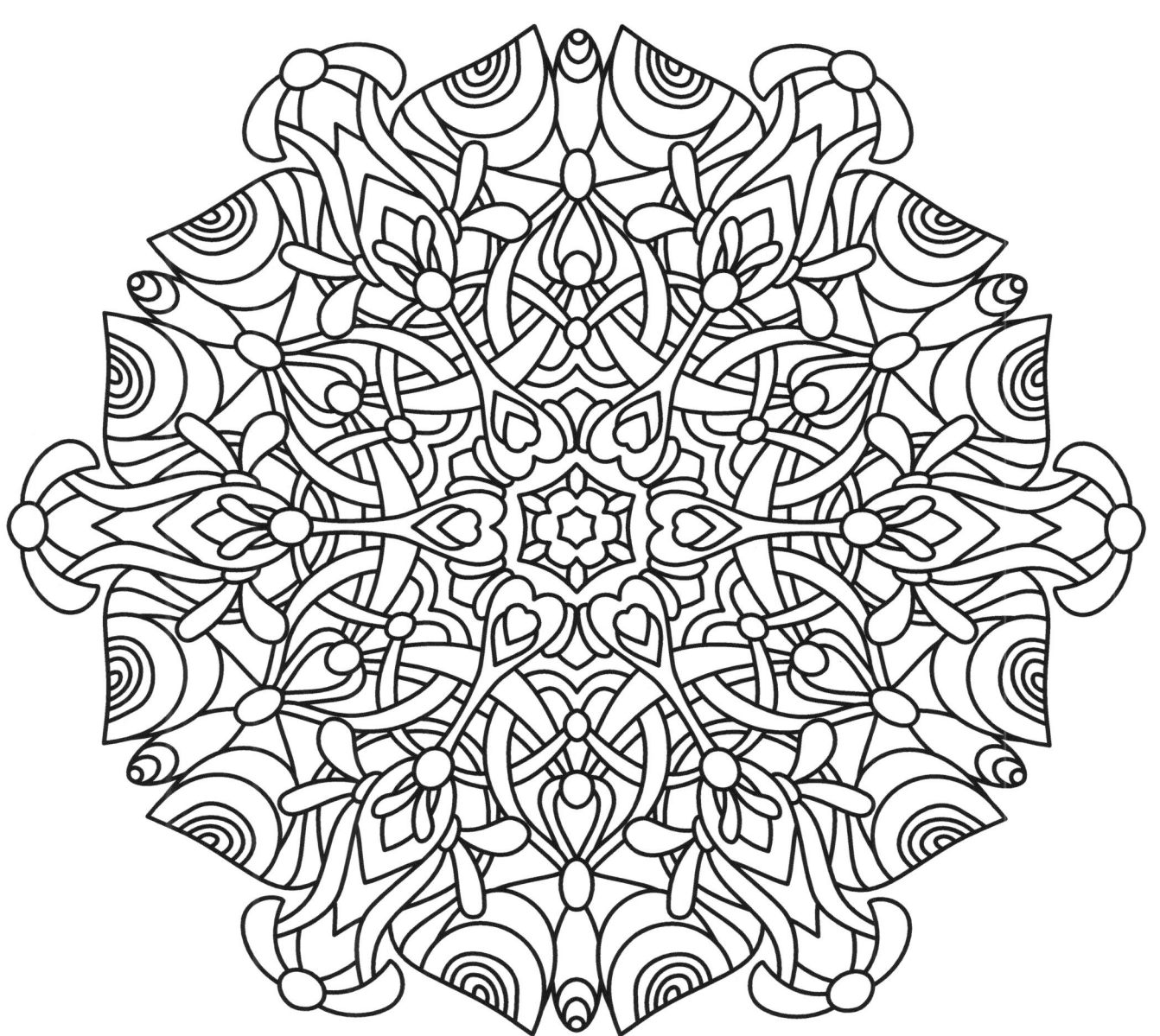

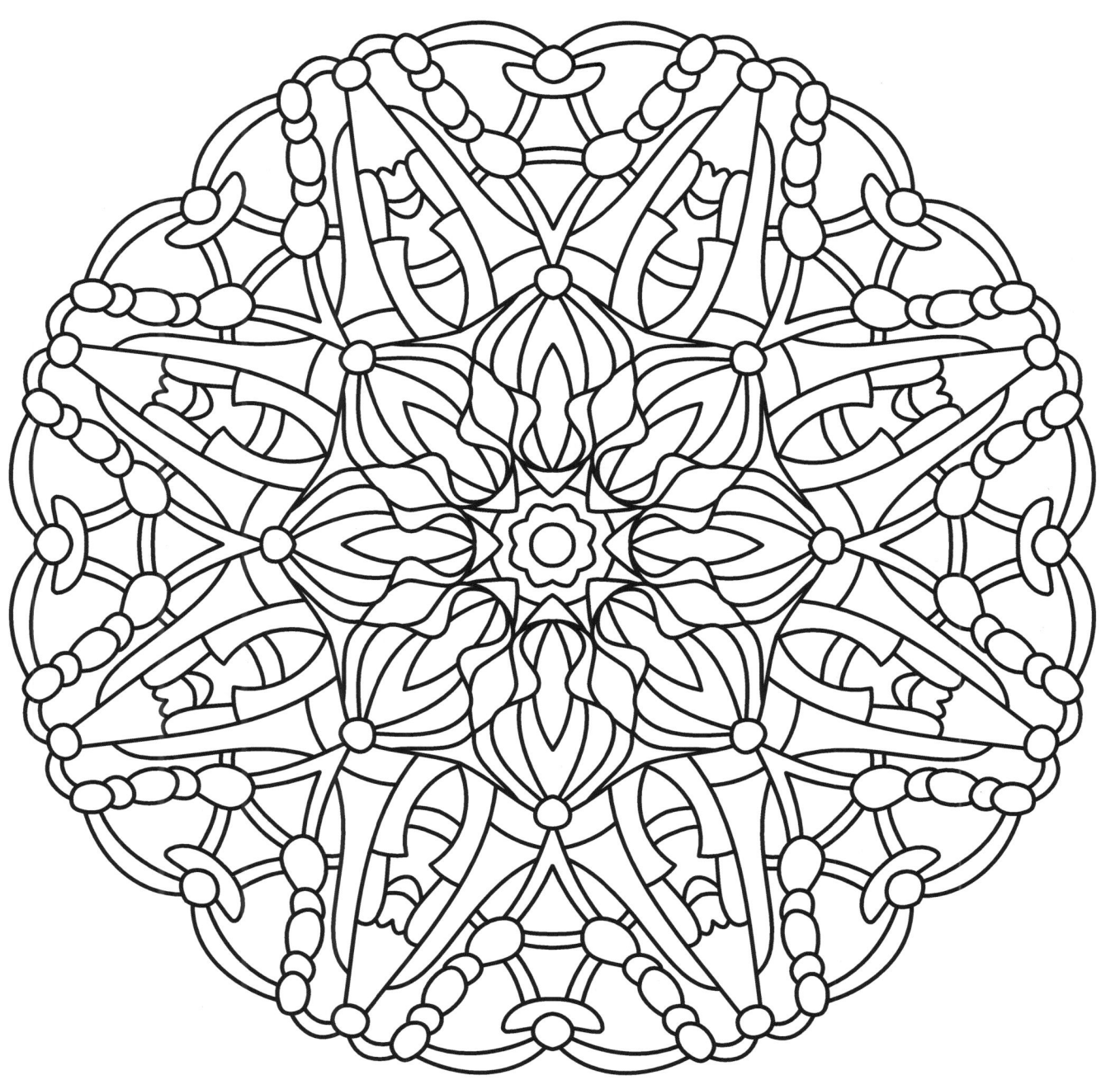

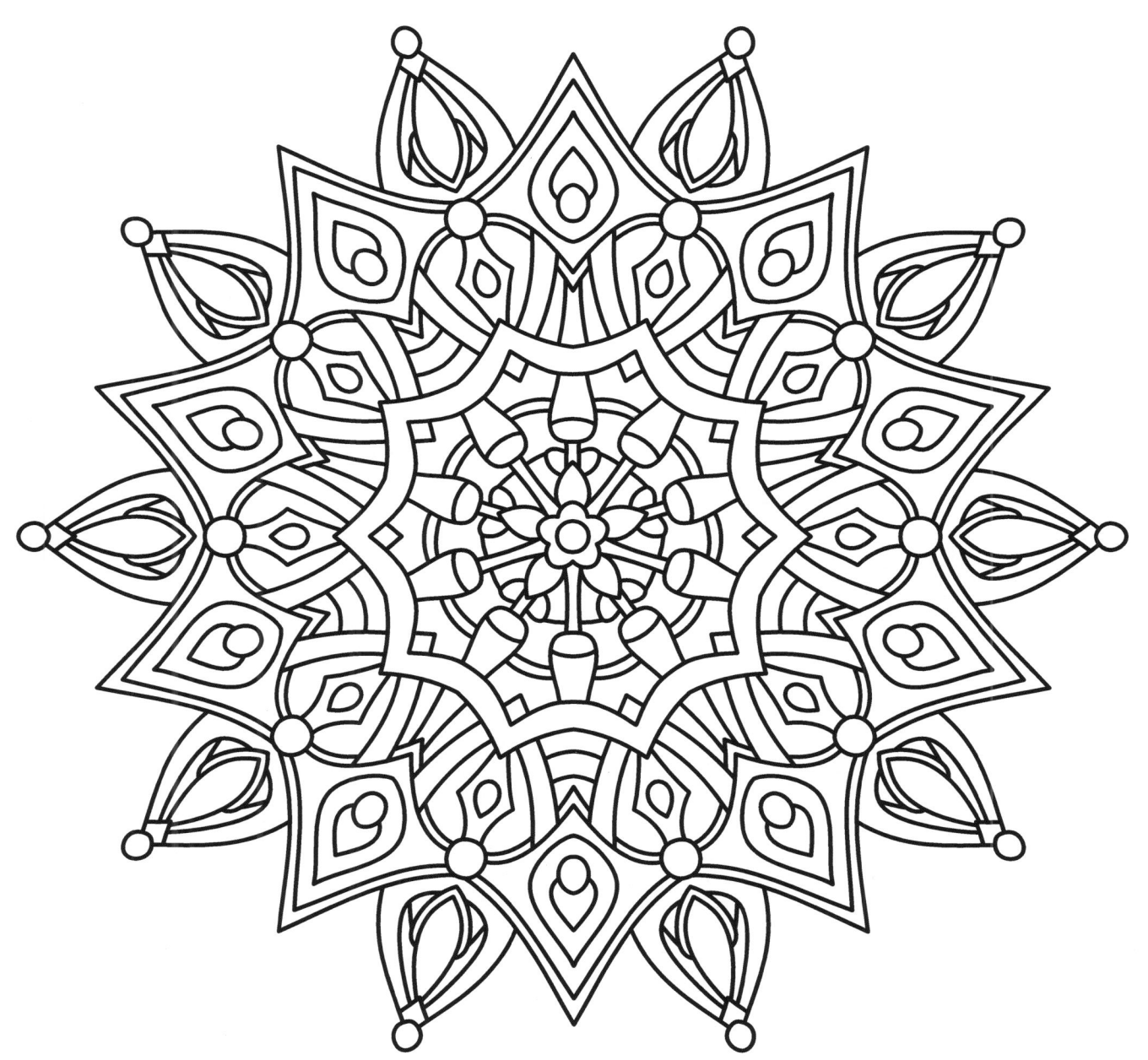

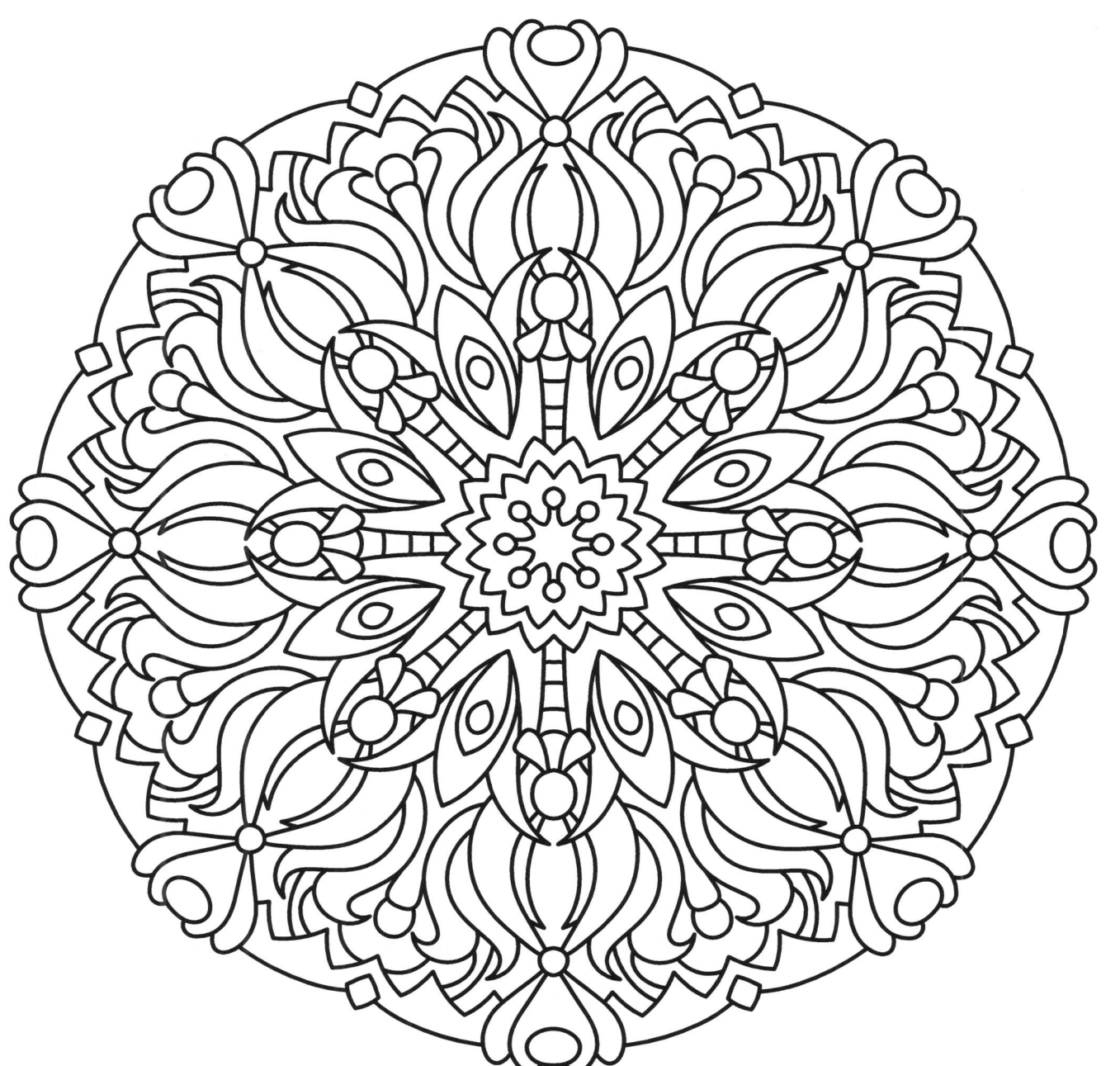

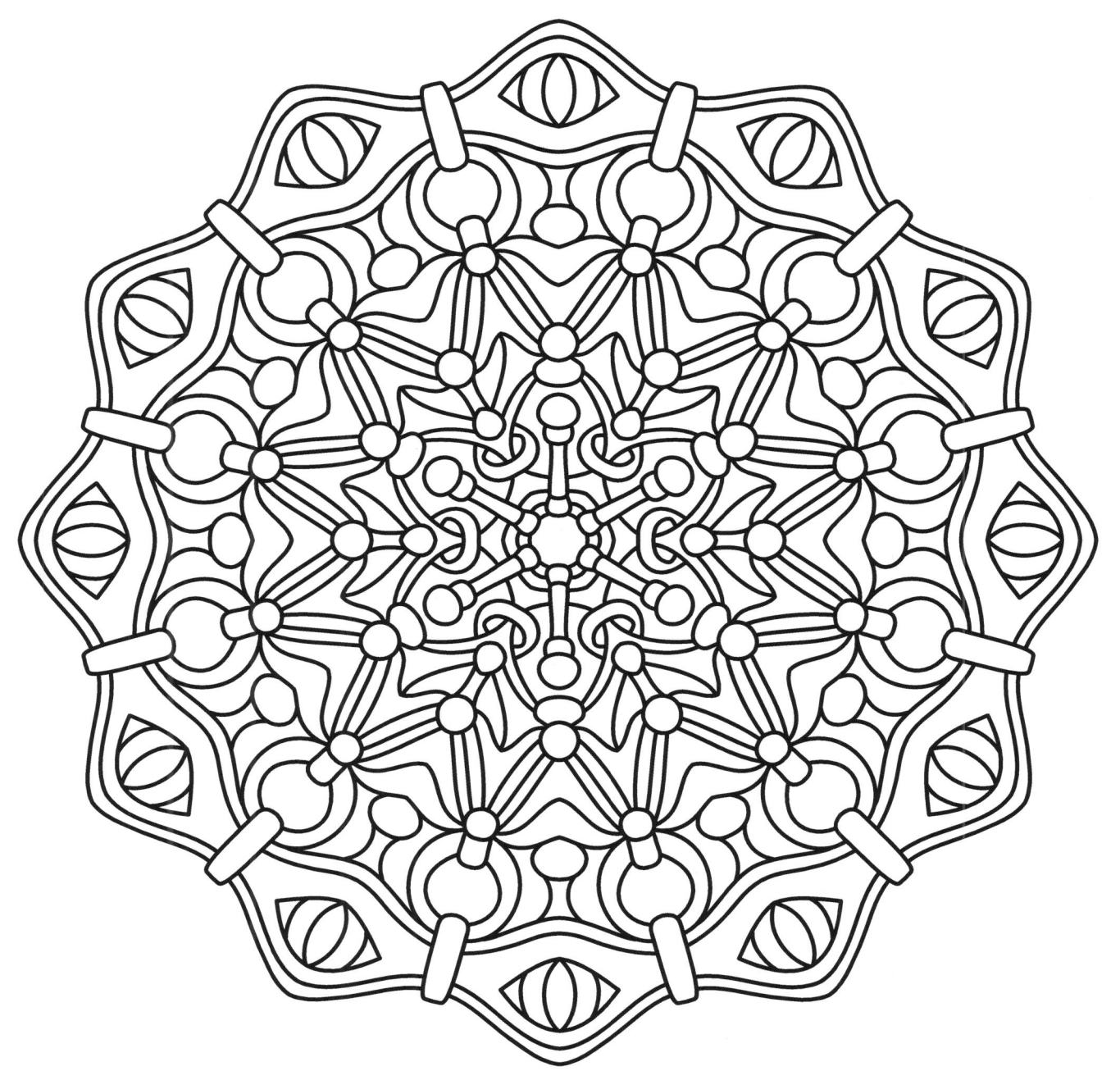

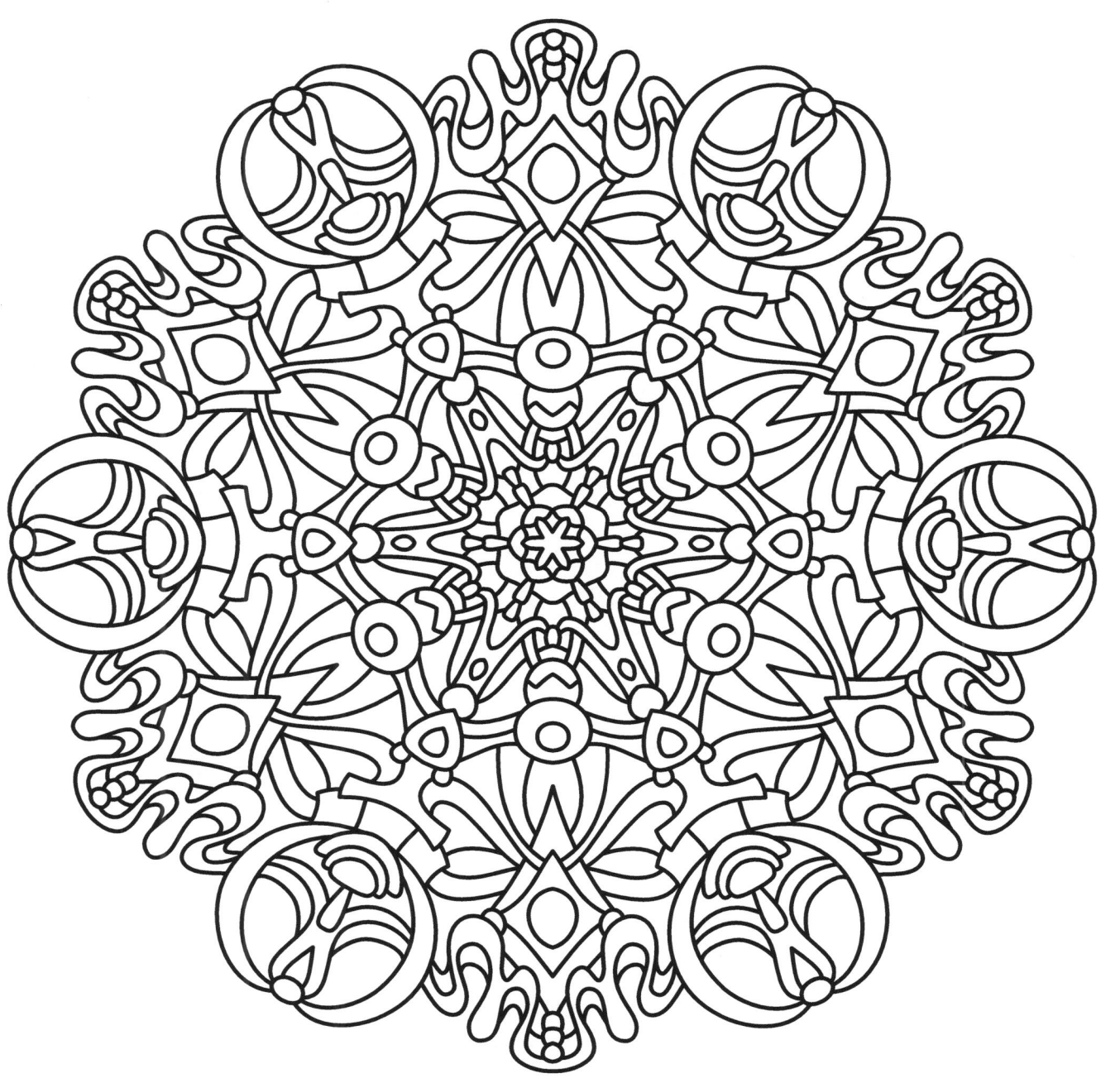

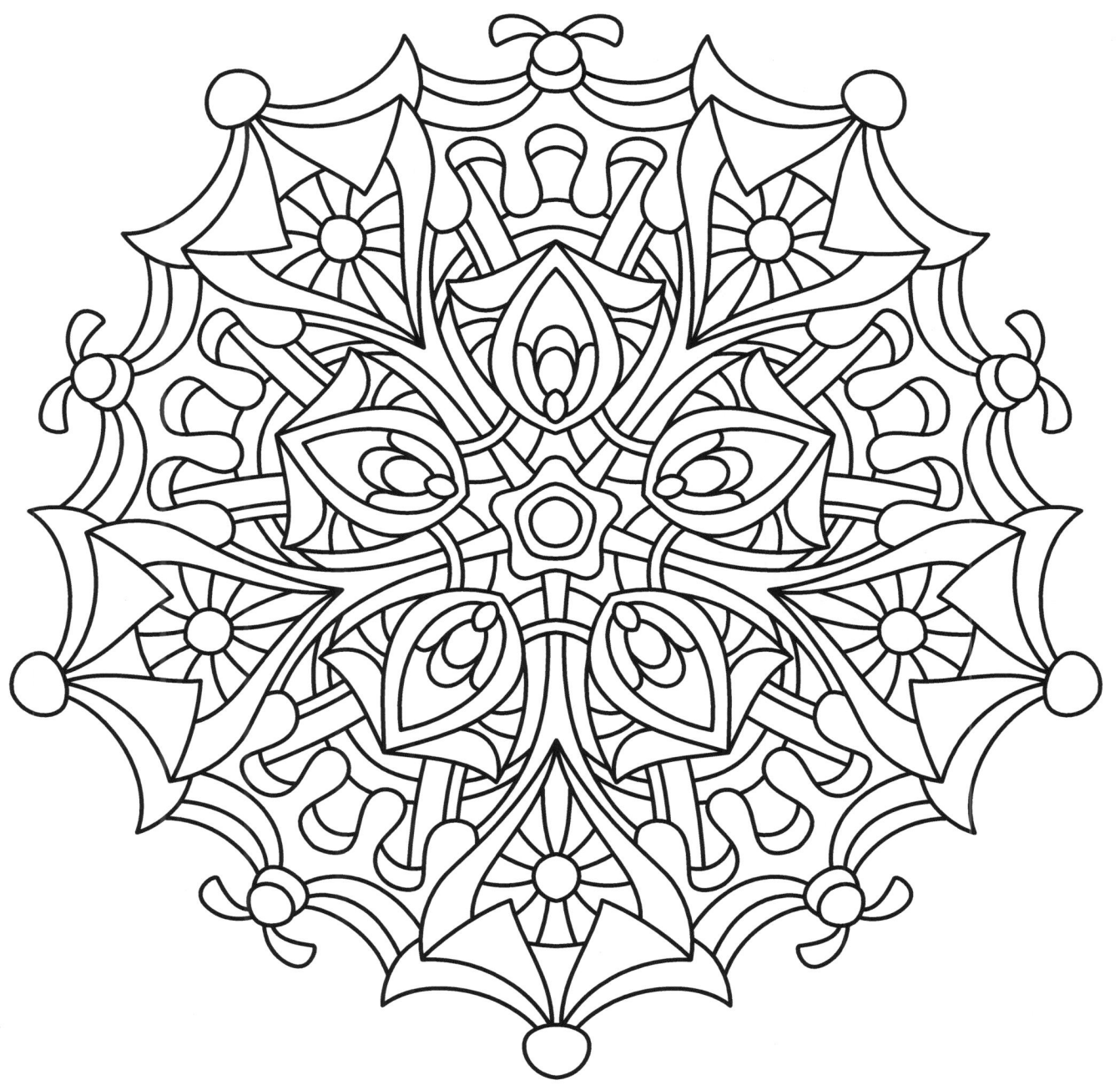

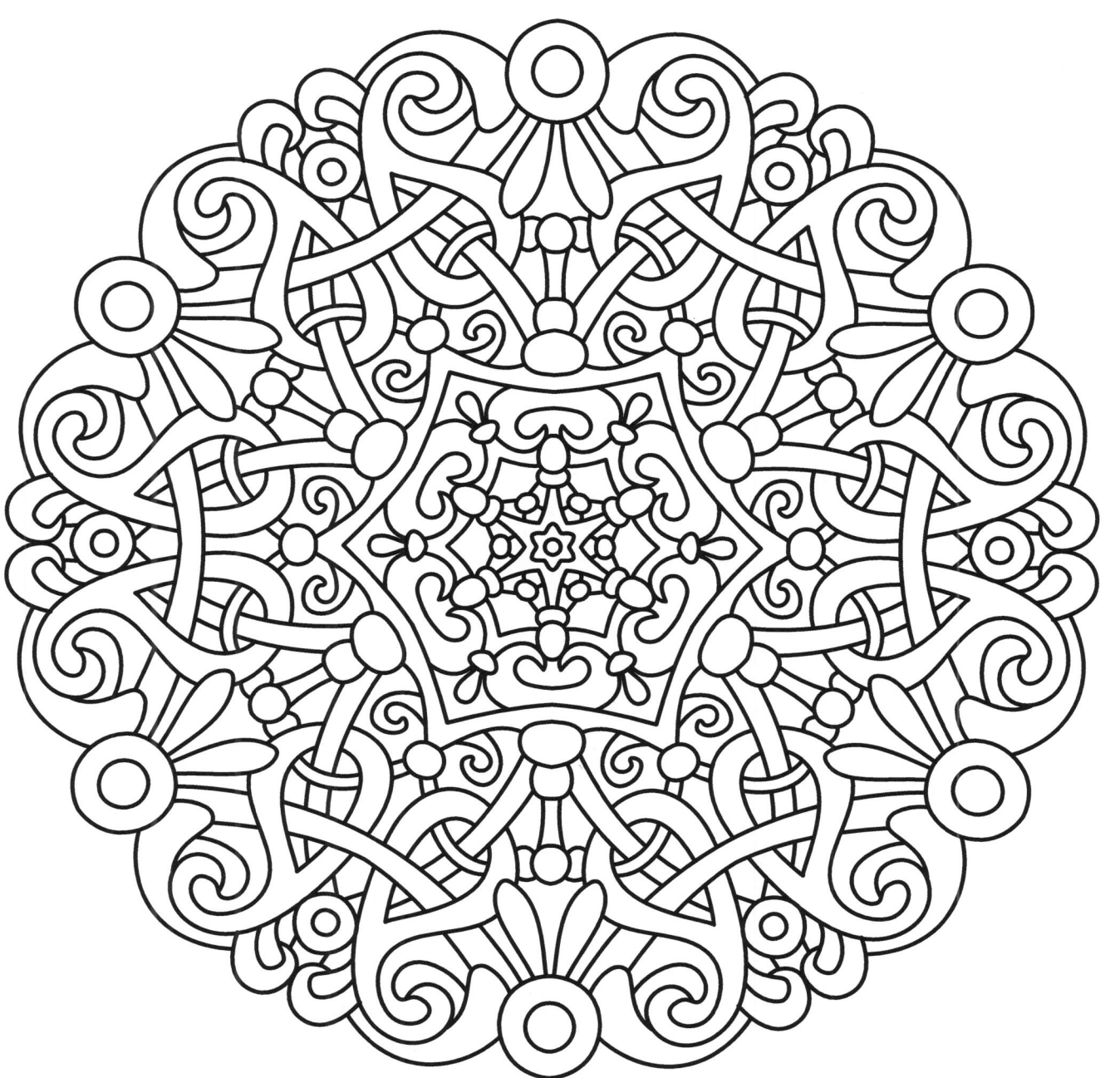

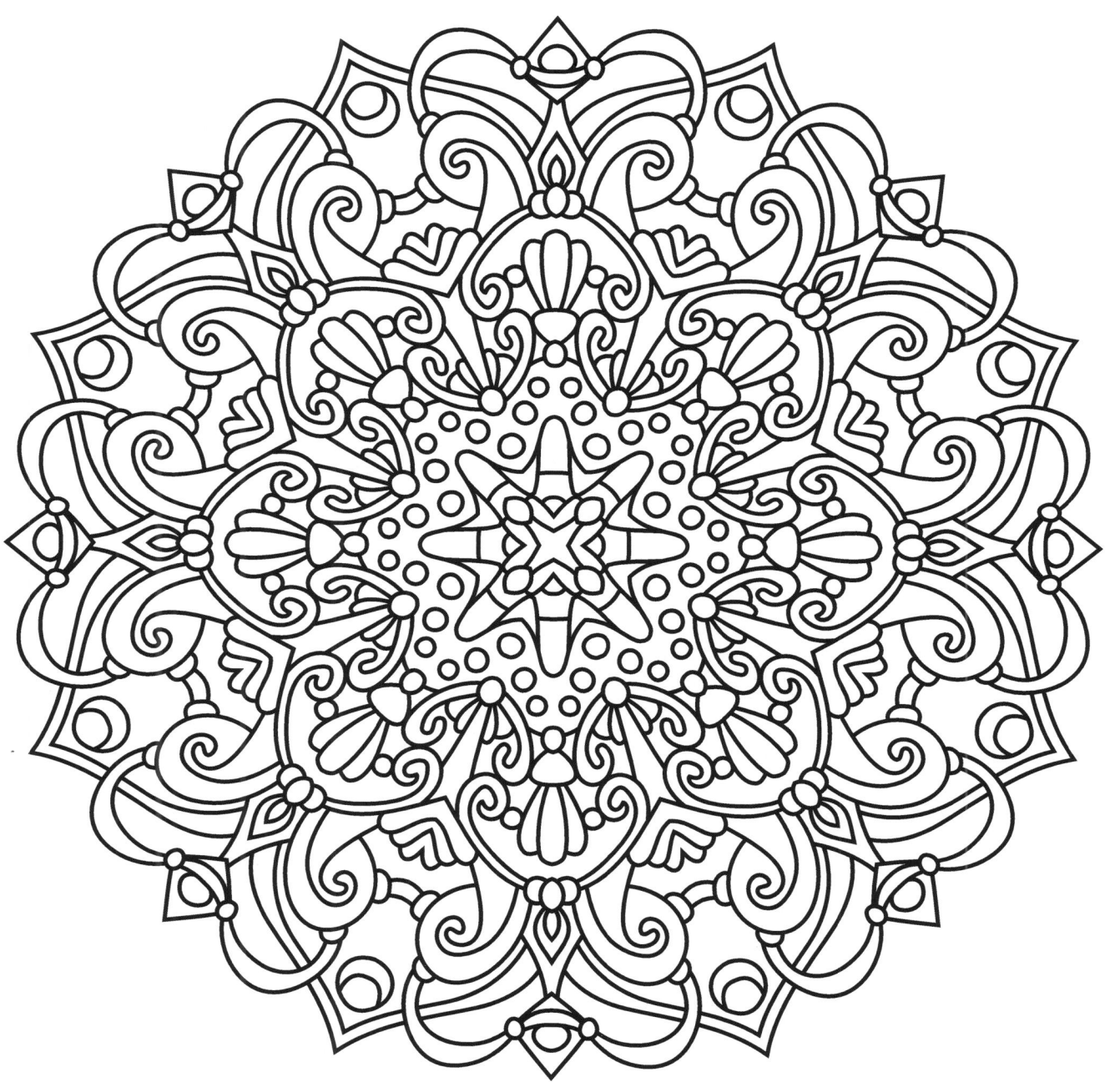

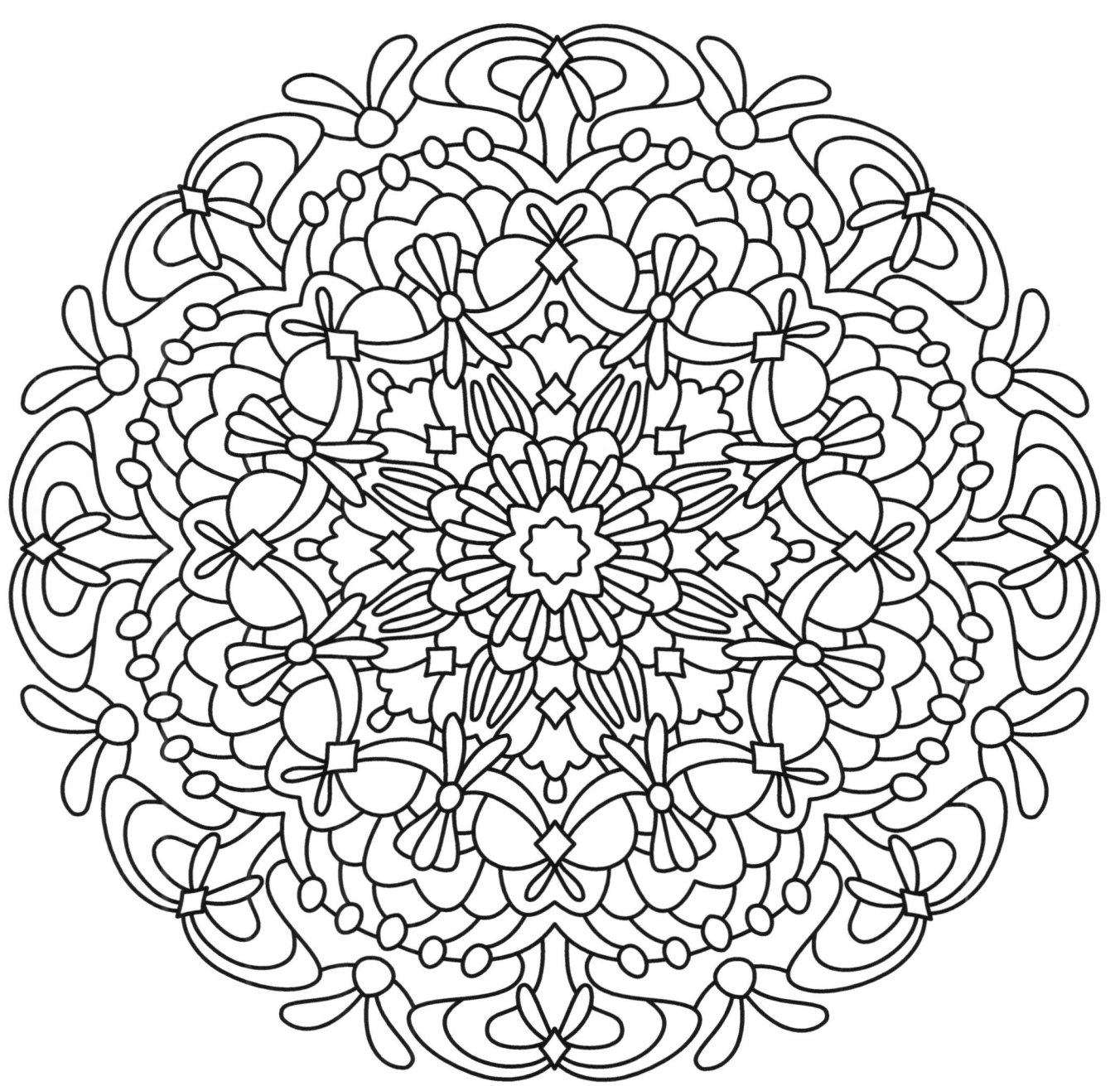

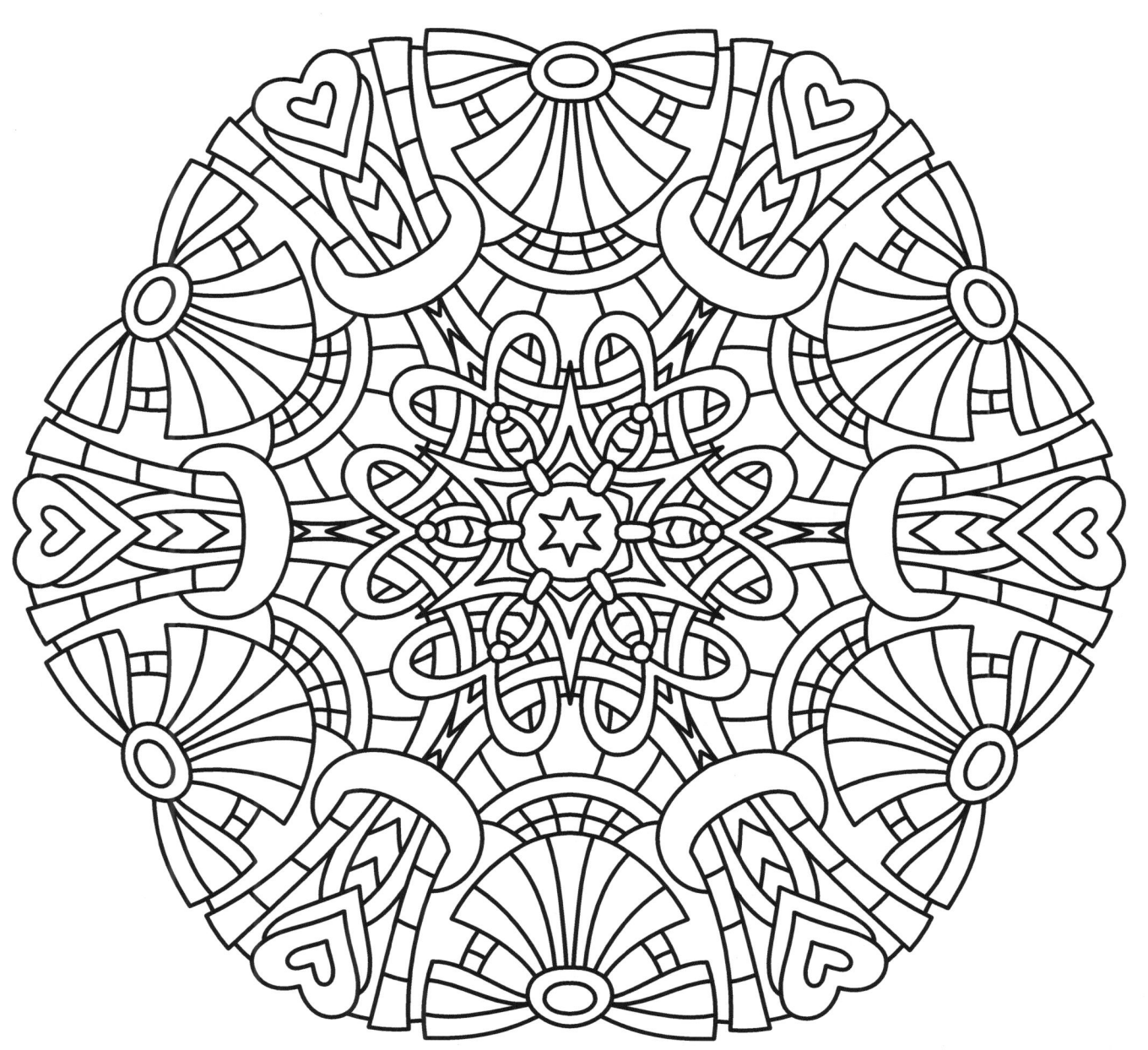

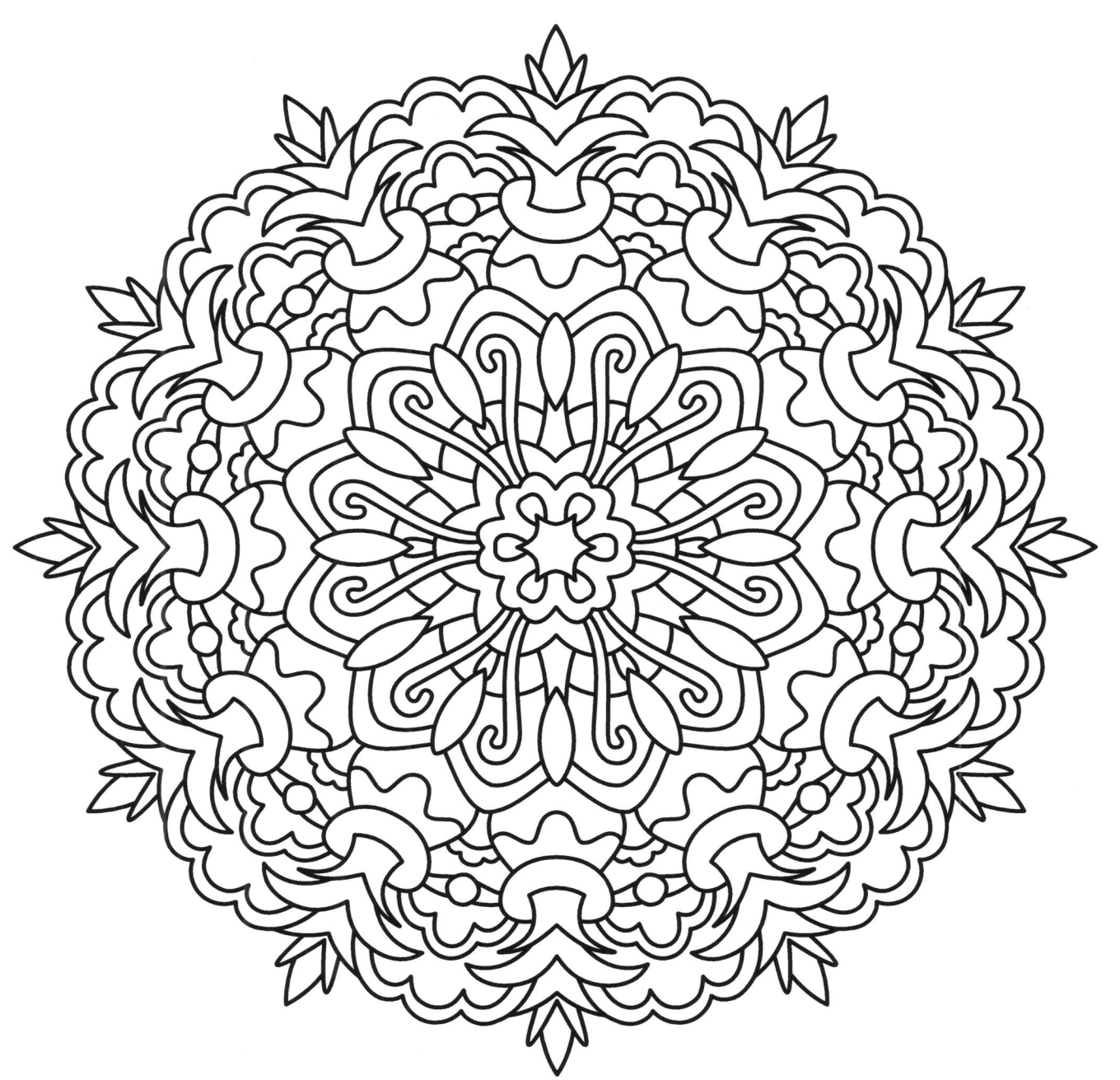

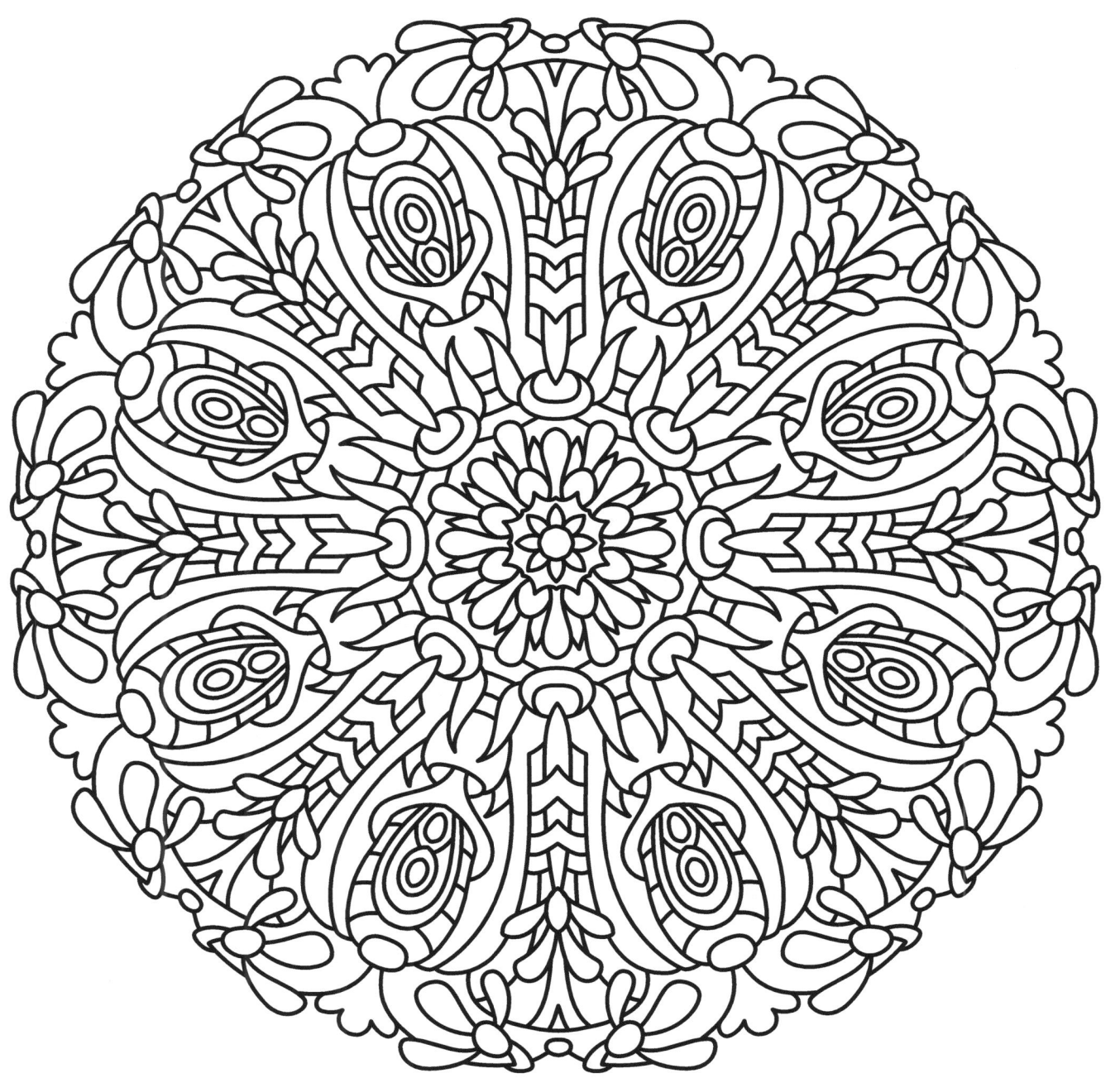

Visit Angie's website
for special web exclusives for colorists.

www.AngieGrace.com

Made in United States
Orlando, FL
09 December 2022

25877527R00057